Gravity and the Creation of Self

Gravity and the Creation of Self

An Exploration of Self-Representations Using Spatial Concepts

Elizabeth Burford

Jessica Kingsley Publishers
London and Philadelphia

Acknowledgement to publishers

Extract from *Playing and Reality* by D. W. Winnicott (1971) reproduced by permission of Mark Paterson on behalf of Routledge and The Winnicott Trust.

Extract from *Through Paediatrics to Psychoanalysis* by D. W. Winnicott (1958) © Clare Winnicott, reproduced by permission of Mark Paterson on behalf of the Hogarth Press and The Winnicott Trust.

Extract from *Schizoid Phenomena, Object Relations and the Self* by Harry Guntrip (1974) © The Estate of Harry Guntrip, reproduced by permission of the Estate of Harry Guntrip on behalf of the Hogarth Press.

Extracts from the writings of Charles Rycroft reprinted by permission of the Peters Fraser and Dunlop Group Ltd.

Poems from *Hot Earth, Cold Earth*, James Berry, [Bloodaxe Books] 1995, by permission of the author and Bloodaxe Books Ltd.

First published in the United Kingdom in 1998 by
Jessica Kingsley Publishers Ltd
116 Pentonville Road
London N1 9JB, England
and
325 Chestnut Street
Philadelphia, PA 19106, U S A

Copyright © 1998 Elizabeth Burford

Library of Congress Cataloging in Publication Data
A CIP catalogue record for this book is available from the Library of Congress

British Library Cataloguing in Publication Data
Gravity and the creation of self: an exploration of self representations using spatial concepts
1.Child psychotherapy 2.Autonomy (Psychology) 3.Space perception in children
I.Title
155.2'5
ISBN 1-85302-557-7

Printed and Bound in Great Britain by
Athenaeum Press, Gateshead, Tyne & Wear

Contents

Figures

To Jane and Anna

Acknowledgements

I am very grateful to Margaret Hodgson, Mollie Dundas, Therese Woodcock and Alison Swan-Parente for their encouragement and advice.

Finally, for dealing with all the complications of information technology, my thanks go to my son-in-law, Trevor Burford-Reade.

Introduction

We live in a three-dimensional world, subject to the force of gravity which grounds us. This force has been one of the main determinants of our physical shape during the evolution of mankind. Spatial concepts are developed as we learn to manoeuvre ourselves around in the real world attempting to satisfy basic needs. These spatial ideas, reflecting a world dominated by the energy force of gravity, are used to place objects, including ourselves, in our version of the concrete world. Because all our activity is in pursuance of some form of satisfaction, value (negative as well as positive) becomes associated with the various spatial positions. These positions are then employed to indicate emotional states. Examples of spatial ideas being used in this way are to be found everywhere, particularly in language, and they are intrinsic to the visual arts. Common parlance is overflowing with terms relating to the human condition in all its vicissitudes that are couched in spatial terms.

Spatial ideas are used to evaluate and describe the emotional aspect of experience in most spheres of human activity, including the practice of psychotherapy. Therapists, and those in treatment, use such terms in the attempt to comprehend and explain the nature of the inner world. The literature of psychotherapy includes terms such as 'container' and 'contained', 'splitting', 'introjection', 'projection', 'integration', 'fragmentation' etc.

The ubiquitous nature of spatial concepts to convey feelings about life and relationships is striking. At a very basic level there is congruence between the experience of the physical condition of maintaining our position and moving around in the three-dimensional gravity-driven world and the experience of complex interactions with those around us. In other words, ideas about gravity are applied to social experience, not just to the purely physical experience of responding to the energy force of gravity. The most disrupting emotions a person can ever experience in life are those elicited in the course of establishing, maintaining and breaking relationships with other people. To convey the impact of such experiences, we invariably use spatial ideas.

Each individual human being works out how best he can manoeuvre himself in the world of objects amongst which he finds himself but one unit. In a reasonably just and equable society a balance is struck between individual needs and those of the wider group. There is a degree of respect both ways.

Unfortunately, this kind of condition does not exist in all groupings of people. Indeed, the larger and more complex a society becomes, the less easy it is for balance to be struck between different parts of the whole organization. Power tends to be wielded with little or no consideration for its impact on those who happen to be passively involved. Whatever the nature of a particular society, each individual member responds by developing characteristic ways of relating to others. If ways of delineating the pattern of the internal world for an individual were found, it would reveal characteristics of their uniquely evolved ways of relating. This patterning, created through interaction with others, has spatial characteristics.

I have confined my attention, as far as possible, to the relevance of spatial ideas in our thinking about ourselves in relationship to our particular social reality. What we refer to as 'the inner world', is the summation of this stored understanding.

The work of Margaret Lowenfeld, as a pioneer of child psychotherapy, is particularly relevant to any discussion about spatial ideas and emotional life. Margaret Mead, in her foreword to the Lowenfeld World Technique book, commented that Margaret Lowenfeld was concerned about 'the insufficiency of words' in self-expression. This remark only partly explains why Lowenfeld went out of her way to provide such a wide range of play materials. But it is a mistake to suggest that she was interested only in 'non-verbal techniques'. She was interested in the totality of the child's behaviour, including what the child had to say.

On the subject of the importance of play for a child, Margaret Lowenfeld said: 'Play is to a child, therefore, work, thought, art, and relaxation, and cannot be pressed into any singular formula. It expresses a child's relation to himself and his environment, and, without adequate opportunity for play, normal and satisfactory emotional development is not possible.' (Lowenfeld 1991, p.232). In this she agreed with Piaget, who said: 'from the point of view of expression itself, the child is midway between the use of the collective sign (i.e. language) and that of the individual symbol, both being necessary, no doubt, but the second being much more so in the child than in the adult' (Piaget 1947, p.159).

Margaret Lowenfeld was a mathematician, to the extent that she was very interested in mathematical ideas and how children developed these notions. She produced a set of special wooden blocks, called Poleidoblocs, to help children discover such ideas for themselves. This equipment is currently being used in schools in the teaching of mathematics. Research is being carried out at Homerton Teacher Training College to find out how it is that children use them to understand mathematical notions. The findings so far show that tactile and other sensory stimuli are very important in the development of these abstract ideas.

Lowenfeld was more fully aware than some that the mode of thinking that embraces spatial ideas is the underlying stratum upon which the verbal faculty works. The quality of this early form of thought determines the nature and form of later logical thought processes.

I have set out a brief description of the two main psychotherapeutic techniques devised by Margaret Lowenfeld: 'The World Technique' and 'The Mosaic Test'. She devised other tools for helping communication between child (or adult) and therapist. The emphasis was less on the emotional relationship between child and therapist than on providing means of self-expression in order to enhance the child's ability to organize and make sense of his or her experience. With these techniques, Lowenfeld produced distinctive theoretical contributions, including the identification of a primary form of thought which she called the 'proto-system':

> This is a system of grouping and linking between experiences, giving rise to primitive thought structures which she called clusters. The proto-system exists before words, is multimodal and multidimensional, and cannot be translated into language. Lowenfeld linked this primitive thought to a fundamental drive to pattern, giving rise to primitive aesthetic awareness. Later she added the theory of E, a neutral force of energy, which gains in strength and polarity according to its relation with structures through which it flows. (Davis and Urwin 1991, p.9)

The Lowenfeld techniques for use in psychotherapy

By way of introduction to the Lowenfeld techniques of psychotherapy, I would like to draw on some ideas about play expressed by Winnicott (1974), as his ideas were close to those of Margaret Lowenfeld. He said that he was reaching towards a new statement about playing and that he was interested in what he found to be a lack of a useful statement on the subject of play in the psychoanalytic literature. Though the different schools of child analysis are built around the child's playing, he found it rather surprising that they make few statements on the general topic of playing. Winnicott said that it is necessary to go to those who are not analysts for this insight.

One book he is referring to is *Play in Childhood* by Lowenfeld (1991). Winnicott comments on the very different way in which an interest in the child's play manifests itself in the writing of Melanie Klein. He suggested that she was more interested in 'the use of play', in so far as she was concerned with play. He goes on to say that 'The therapist is reaching for the child's communication and knows that the child does not usually possess the command of language that can convey the infinite subtleties that are to be found in play by those who seek.' (1974, p.46)

Whilst disclaiming any criticism of Melanie Klein, or others, he continues:

It is simply a comment on the possibility that in the total theory of the personality the psychoanalyst has been too busy using play content to look at the playing child, and to write about playing as a thing in itself. It is obvious that I am making a significant distinction between the noun 'play' and the verbal noun 'playing'. (Winnicott 1974, p.46)

The chapter continues with the theme 'Playing in Time and Space'. Winnicott postulates 'a potential space' between mother and baby which varies according to the life experience of the baby in relation to the mother. He states his aim as being to draw attention away from 'sequence psychoanalysis', by which I assume he means the linear quality that is the tendency of classical analysis. Though adult communication is usually verbal, these ideas about playing are equally applicable to adults.

In exploring ideas about play, he says that he is looking instead to 'play that is universal, and that belongs to health: playing facilitates growth and therefore health; playing leads into group relationships; playing can be a form of communication in psychotherapy...' (Winnicott 1974, p.48) He points out that playing is a natural thing, whilst psychoanalysis is a highly specialized sophisticated form of playing in the service of communication with oneself and others.

Winnicott presents many illustrations of playing taking place between himself and the child in psychotherapy. 'It is good to remember always that playing is itself a therapy.' (p.58) He also makes statements about the use of play, which some might find controversial but which would be in tune with the Lowenfeldian approach to psychotherapy that places 'playing' at the heart of the process. The following is particularly apt in considering the Lowenfeld approach:

...the therapist is concerned specifically with the child's own growth processes and with the removal of blocks to development that may have become evident. It is psychoanalytic theory that has made for an understanding of these blocks. At the same time it would be a narrow view to suppose that psychoanalysis is the only way to make use of child's playing. (Winnicott 1974, p.58)

The essential feature of my communication is this, that playing is an experience, always a creative experience, and it is an experience in the space-time continuum, a basic form of living. (p.59)

Like Lowenfeld, Winnicott believed that play was a vitally important activity for the child and that playing itself had therapeutic effects. As an intensely creative experience, taking place in time and space, it has everything in it. For this reason, he understood that psychotherapy of a deep-going kind may be done without interpretative work.

The psychotherapist may also work on the material, the content of playing. But, as Winnicott pointed out, during therapeutic consultations, the significant moment comes when the child surprises himself or herself after playing creatively. He placed less emphasis than some analysts on clever interpretation.

As a further endorsement of the importance of the area of overlap of the patient's and the analyst's (or therapist's) playing together, he says that interpretation outside the ripeness of the material is indoctrination and causes compliance. A corollary is that resistance arises out of interpretation given outside the area of overlap of the patient's and the analyst's playing together. The quality of this 'playing together' depends on a deep feeling of trust, akin to the early close relationship between mother and child.

In her work with children exhibiting emotional/behavioural difficulties, Margaret Lowenfeld made the close observation and study of the child playing the starting point of her work. She had explored a wide range of theories about the development of the psyche. She began to work out her own theoretical approach to psychotherapy in the light of a broad interest in human affairs. She emphasised the importance of ensuring that theoretical considerations never came to dominate clinical material. She focused on the fact that each child (or adult) is a unique individual. She was at pains to understand each child in the light of his or her own particular expressions alongside the child's developmental history and background.

In her exploratory work with individual children she provided a wide range of objects, materials and situations for the child to use. By so doing, she facilitated the child's ability to recreate, in a subtle way, complex and difficult ideas. It is impressive to see just how selective children can be, given a wide range of play materials, when focused on the serious process of psychotherapy. They frequently make unusual choices of objects, and of combinations of objects, in order to create some quite special effect to express a particular idea. As Margaret Mead said of Lowenfeld (1977): 'She developed instruments of communication which did not depend on verbalization' and 'she was most of all preoccupied with the insufficiency of words to express those aspects of childhood thought and feeling which interested her most.' (p.vii)

Lowenfeld explained her purpose in setting up the world technique:

> My own endeavour in my work with children is to devise an instrument with which a child can demonstrate his own emotional and mental state without the necessary intervention of an adult either by transference or interpretation, and which will allow a record being made of such a demonstration. My objective is to help children to produce something which will stand by itself and will be independent of any theory as to its nature. (1977, p.3)

She said that her approach to the use of toy apparatus derived from a memory of H.G.Wells' *Floor Games*, the first edition of which had made a deep impression on her.

The Lowenfeld World Technique

Basic concept

The basis of the World apparatus is to provide the maker with tools of a multidimensional 'language', an essential and unique quality of which is the power to facilitate expression of concepts and of inner experience which are outside the framework of even 'fantastic' drawing and modelling, although no special skill in the maker is demanded.

The tools

1. A tray for dry sand – approximately 75cm x 52cm with a depth of 7cm.

2. A waterproof tray for damp sand – the same size as above.

3. A good supply of dry sand. Facilities should be provided to make possible the use of more or less sand, together with funnels, sieves, containers etc. Sand has the propensity to represent other material objects or symbolize subtle, abstract ideas. It was found to be important to provide an arbitrary boundary for this technique (as well as for the Lowenfeld Mosaic Test). The frame focuses the attention and limits the output of the maker at any one session. The tray should be placed on a table of a height suitable for the maker.

4. Water should be available, together with cans, jugs and tools such as wooden spoons, shovels etc.

5. A box of amorphous objects. This should contain bricks, rubber tubes of various lengths and widths, small shallow tins (for making ponds etc.), coloured sticks and slats etc.

6. A cabinet for World objects. This should contain shallow drawers to display most of the World objects. The collection of World objects should be as wide as possible according to what is available at any given time.

7. Miniature objects of the following kinds: living creatures – ordinary men, women and children, soldiers, entertainers, people of other races, wild and domestic animals; fantasy and folk-lore figures and animals, including prehistoric and 'space' specimens; scenery – buildings of any kind, trees, bushes, flowers, fences, gates and bridges; transport – for road, rail, sea and air; equipment – for road, town, farms and gardens, playground and fairs, hospital, school; miscellaneous objects – which may be anything available.

Record keeping of Worlds

The recording of Worlds is vitally important during a course of therapy. Lowenfeld decided that a diagrammatic drawing of a World, done on the spot, usually by the therapist, is the most satisfactory recording method. Such a drawing makes possible an equal emphasis on all objects, whatever their position in the tray. Perspective drawing and photography have the disadvantage of giving too much emphasis to objects in the foreground.

The Lowenfeld Mosaic Test

For a fuller description of this test, there is a handbook from the Lowenfeld Trust by Anderson and Hood-Williams (n.d.), from which quotations, below, have been made.

The test material consists of a box of flat coloured plastic pieces and a tray... (lined with a sheet of white paper to record the pattern) in which the pattern is made.

Unlike all other instruments for the investigation of mental functioning, the Lowenfeld Mosaic Test is almost entirely non-verbal. Words are needed when giving the instructions and when enquiring about the meaning for the subject of his response.

The task for the subject is to create meaning from an extensive but nevertheless limited range of only minimally meaningful material, and he must do this within a defined and limited space – the area of the paper on the tray.

He must structure the material available, and since he can only do this in accord with the principles of his own mental structuring, in making his response to the test he provides the tester with information about how he functions in a wide range of areas of his personality.

The Lowenfeld Mosaic Test thus can provide a range of information about a subject which differs significantly from the information provided by other tests. It can be used alone or in conjunction with other tests and it has the further advantage of being only minimally affected by practice effects should repeat – testing be required. Uniquely it provides an opportunity to observe the personality in spontaneous action.

Observing the making of a Mosaic

'The tester should record in as much detail as possible the making of the Mosaic', the processes by which the self-representation is made. Various aspects of the whole process are worth noting, such as the attitude to the task, the manner of carrying it out, the position of the starting point and the direction of growth of the design; did the pattern develop from the centre outwards, from the outside inwards, upwards, downwards, symmetrically, asymmetrically, randomly, haphazardly or showing conflicting tendencies? Other things worth noting concern changes such as false starts, abrupt changes, many or few changes during construction. Finally, what is the subject's response to the finished product – if indeed it was considered to be finished?

Uses of the Mosaic test

1. As an expressive medium: 'This is most apparent when the test is used in psychotherapy. Patients may use it repeatedly once they have discovered it's value as a medium for non-verbal expression of aspects of themselves they find are inaccessible in other media'.

2. Diagnostically it has two main areas of application: 'It can be used in a manner analogous to other tests as an aid to understanding disturbances of functioning, be they emotional, educational or social'. The other use is to monitor the ongoing process, for example psychotherapy, remedial education, etc. 'Mosaics made at intervals will indicate progress, lack of progress, or deterioration.'

Understanding Mosaic designs depends partly on developing a conceptual framework as a tool for thinking about the meaning of a Mosaic. It does not provide clear-cut answers. It could be said that the term 'test' applied here is misleading. Tests usually provide just that, clear-cut results, but, in this case, the Lowenfeld Mosaic opens up fresh vistas on the individual being tested.

The tester must be able to look objectively at the design he is presented with. He then needs to think about it within a framework of ideas that relates to the whole broad spectrum of what it is possible to make with the Lowenfeld Mosaic Test pieces. The Mosaic Test poses questions for which the tester must search for answers within the Mosaic itself. At best, it provides only a range of indicators, signposts as it were, which help the tester towards making a formulation about the subject.

There are no incontrovertible conclusions to be drawn from features of a particular mosaic pattern. For example, it would be untrue to deduce that because a subject uses black he is depressed or 'patterns attached to the rim of the tray mean that the subject suffers from insecurity.' The Mosaic test is a tool for the exploration of personality and interpretations of this kind are far too rigid.

Imagery in the form of the Lowenfeld Mosaics is an effective way of gaining insight into the internal world of an individual at a particular time in a particular social context. One example was given in an earlier section: a 'hanging down' mosaic was made by a dependent boy who had been prevented from developing confidence by over-protective, domineering parents. A very different form of mosaic would be a centralized, well organized pattern, suggesting that the character structure of the person who made it was strong and independent. The reverse would be true of a person who created a pattern which was mainly attached to the sides of the tray (representing external forces), particularly if the central area was empty – revealing the insecurity about the self and difficulty in acting independently.

The nature of the pattern and the manner in which it was constructed, against a background of information about the social environment, provides a basis for ongoing exploration, with the creator of the mosaic, of the way in which he or she is attempting to cope with reality. Insight into the self-image of the creator, and, probably, some notion of the relative strength of internal and external forces, is often suggested by the form of the pattern and the way in which it fits into the space.

Features of the Mosaic may indicate disturbance

1. 'Where the Mosaic presents a scene, image or concept indicative in itself of disturbance.'

2. Where a part of the human figure is distorted or over-emphasized.

3. 'Representations of buildings or structures which should be stable or in movement, but which give a strong impression of instability or of falling to pieces.'

4. Certain types of abstract designs provide pointers to disturbance, for example an unsuccessful attempt to cover the whole tray.

5. Disturbance may be indicated within the structure of a design, for example where there is an empty space at the centre of an abstract design or where the pattern forms a cross.

6. The use of colour is subject to cultural differences. However, there may be pointers to disturbance in the way colours are used: excessive use of black (apart from its use to emphasize other colours) can be an indicator of depression.

7. Excessive use of white, particularly in an abstract design, either at the centre or at the periphery, can be an indication of diminished self-esteem, or poor capacity to relate to others or to work.

8. 'Strongly contrasting combinations of red and black, particularly at the centre of abstract designs are pointers towards difficulties in relation to anger and aggression.' (see figures on pp.32–3)

Both of the Lowenfeld techniques (Worlds and Mosaics) may be used in diagnosis and, at the same time, they have therapeutic value. Therefore, at the initial diagnostic interview, they are useful alongside other information such as the social and medical history, intelligence tests, etc. Whether or not to use either of these techniques is always a matter of choice for the individual (patient). Where they are enjoyed as a means of self-expression, further use of the World Technique or the Mosaic test, after the initial diagnostic interview, may become one of the main focuses during a course of treatment.

Spatial and verbal forms of thinking

Early learning during the period when the child is totally dependent on others will, at its best, create a sense of wholeness which also entails a sense of separateness. This sense of emotional well-being is the basis for the development of integrity and the capacity to think intelligently and to behave in a creative manner. Early learning is predominantly involved with spatial ideas. Verbal thinking develops at a later stage, but the two forms of thought are different aspects of the whole process. The intimate connection between thinking and feeling also needs stressing.

Current thinking throws light on the complementary nature of spatial (concrete) and verbal (abstract) thinking. Foundations for the underlying global form of thinking are laid down early in life. The soundness of the structure depends largely on the quality of nurturing. In later life we are largely unaware of how much our thinking has been influenced by our early experiences. Spatial and verbal forms of thinking are two integrated aspects of the enormously complex working of the brain.

The dichotomy usually emphasized between abstract and concrete intelligence has been misleading because there is, in fact, an intimate connection between form perception and the process of abstraction linked to verbalization.

Guidano (1987) discusses how these two functions, spatial and verbal thinking, are predominantly located on different sides of the brain. The right hemisphere is more concerned with holistic and synthetic time/space relationships – that is with the processing of unconscious, tacit information. The left hemisphere is specialized for sequential and analytic processes and, in particular, for language. The way in which the two functions differ from each other whilst operating together in a complex manner is only just beginning to be understood. (pp. 18–19)

The value which Margaret Lowenfeld placed upon children's play means that the two forms of thinking may be seen operating together. Play is a multi-dimensional event, quite different from words alone. Play also needs to be put in a wider context. Here is a passage (written by Margaret Mead) from the foreword to *The World Technique*:

> ...she [Margaret Lowenfeld] combined her insights from treating sick children with insights gained from an enthusiastic inquiry into the history of civilisation, the contrasts between different cultures and the special creativity of artists, poets and great religious leaders. She was one of the first to realise that the special kinds of thought which are manifestations of early childhood perceptions of the world are not only the roots of trouble in disturbed children, but also the precious precursors of the work of genius. (Lowenfeld 1977, p.vii)

Each individual creates within himself, during the process of adaptation to his own particular setting, a unique, many-faceted (psychic) pattern. These self-representations are based on relationships within our different life experiences, i.e. within the family and social structure which has supported us (or failed to do so). Our knowledge of ourselves is shaped by the nature of such interchanges.

D'Arcy Wentworth Thompson (1942) explored patterns to be found in the natural world in his book *On Growth and Form*. They were developed by organisms living on earth through adaptation to the material world dominated by gravity. In a similar way, psychic patterns develop which underlie thinking and give rise to the definitive characteristics of personality. Of course, internal patterning is not observable directly, as are the patterns created by plant growth, but both kinds of pattern are created in relation to such factors as gravity and light in the physical world. Internal patterns, also created during the process of adaptation, are equally real though less tangible. They constitute an enduring, though malleable, structure which has been constructed in response to interactions in the three-dimensional world of objects – primarily those of human beings – whose support is crucial to survival. So long as interaction continues, modification of the internal pattern is possible. It should not be assumed that these developments or modifications are always beneficial for the individual or his environment. They may be helpful for survival in the short term but disastrous in the long term.

In this book I have extracted the spatial elements from the wealth of expressive material, some of which was produced during psychotherapy. I have grouped the ideas and attempted to arrange them in some kind of order.

Two spatial dimensions of our internal organisation have been identified as being of particular importance

The first is related to awareness of the up/down axis as a result of the need to resist the pull of gravity. Much physical effort is expended, accommodating to the effects of gravity, on our essential movements and the need to maintain an advantageous position in space. Success or failure in doing so produces a strong emotional reaction. Purely interpersonal experiences are also the source of similar strong emotional reactions. Ideas about manoeuvring ourselves in the concrete world, together with their accompanying feelings, are transferred, as appropriate, to the social sphere. Briefly, feeling high equates with success in both aspects (access to resources, power and happiness), while feeling low equates with failure (privation, weakness and sadness).

The second aspect of internal spatial organization is the degree to which a sense of wholeness develops in infancy, starting at the oral level. Good continuous relationships with those upon whom we depend during the vulnerable nurturing situation produces 'containment' and the experience of being 'held', which are vital in the process of creating a sense of wholeness.

Both these dimensions of internal organization, awareness of the up/down axis and a sense of wholeness, are interdependent. Much of the time they appear to exist together in a state of tension, if not in conflict. What happens in the early months and years, when the individual is vulnerable and totally dependent, is vitally important.

To become a 'whole' individual there needs to be a good measure of confidence in one's own capacity or ability to exercise 'power' in order to satisfy one's own needs. A strong sense of self, represented by an upright, forms the core central to the process of becoming whole. But, at the same time, the sense of individual power needs to be integrated and moderated by an appreciation of dependency and the existence of other people's interests if it is not to become over-weaning or destructive.

One way of looking at the work of psychotherapy is in terms of linking, which helps the individual to establish or re-create a degree of wholeness. Margaret Lowenfeld used the term 'cluster' to refer to a complex of thoughts and feelings, which, if focused on painful experience, obliterates or distorts the essential unity of structure which exists. Without this sense of wholeness, there can be no autonomy or settled sense of being able to move in a 'forward' direction. The aim of psychotherapy is to uncover such a 'cluster' of ideas which blocks the integrating process. By working through these restrictive ideas, the aim is to make it possible for the integrating growth process to take over so that energy may be directed more effectively.

Throughout this book mention will be made of expressions from art and literature which have resonance with images produced by children in treatment.

CHAPTER 1

Gravity and the upright position

Gravity being such an all-pervasive force shaping our world, it is not surprising that the up/down dimension is of primary importance. Feelings of extreme well-being produce ideas about being 'high' or 'elated', or of 'walking on air' or 'walking tall'. In contrast, being 'down' conveys the feeling of things going wrong, for example feeling 'run down' or 'put down' or suffering a 'breakdown'. Whether 'high' or 'low', the causation of such extreme states of mind is less likely to be purely physical than to result from satisfied or unsatisfied relationships.

A full engagement with life, in terms of growth and power, is generally associated with the upward movement. In Western capitalist society in particular, where competitive individuality is fostered, the notion of upward movement denotes increased personal power and status, whereas movement downwards denotes its loss. Personal feelings of power, in terms of being able to choose freely whether to act and what action to take, can only operate in social situations where such activity is allowed by institutionalized power structures.

It is interesting to note that in Japan there is a saying: 'When a nail stands up it will always be hammered down'. This confirms the idea that Japanese society is less individualistic and that the social forces producing a sense of interdependency (which also demands a high degree of conformity) are much stronger. This kind of social cohesion may be the determining factor in ensuring that the high level of discrepancy in the distribution of wealth that exists in the United States would not be tolerated in Japan.

Obvious examples of how the up/down dimension represents grades of power are the symbolic use of the ladder and the pyramid to represent the hierarchy of social status. Those at the base, who may not have managed to get a foothold on the lower rungs of the social ladder, may feel themselves to be at 'the bottom of the heap'. Indeed, those higher up the social ladder are likely to confirm this idea by their attitude towards them.

Those looked down upon will also be aware of the fact that those higher up have better access to the source of supplies necessary to provide energy for life and scope for a wider choice of action. Usually, individuals who find themselves in this position make great efforts to 'get out from under'. Such spatial ideas are embedded in the language. Words such as 'submit' and 'subject', when used in a social sense, have combined spatial and political meaning.

The attainment and maintenance of the upright position

The erect living object on earth uses energy from within itself to defy the downward pull of gravity. Gravity is a little-understood source of energy which shapes the whole universe. Whatever its wider significance, it is true that the earth's larger land animals live their lives against the pull of gravity. From the experiential point of view it is of all-pervasive importance. Though we are barely aware of this unseen force working its effect upon us, all our experiences have the imprint of the structure that it imposes. The attainment of erect posture accrues emotional significance and comes in itself to symbolize individuality, integrity and power.

The neurological complexity of being able to stand upright on two legs is enormous, given the small base and the fact that the upright is hinged in more than one place. So far, scientists have been unable to create a robot with only two legs. The gravitational force is felt at a barely conscious level but, from time to time, we are made aware of its effects on our body. An astronaut, when removed from the pull of gravity, eventually loses the muscular strength required to stand up.

During growth and physical development the child gradually gains the muscular power to move from the relatively passive horizontal position to the increasingly independent perpendicular. First, the child learns to lift up the head, later to sit with the torso erect. Then, after usually moving through the crawling stage, the fully erect standing position is attained. Sustained muscular effort over a long period of time goes into this achievement, which clearly produces a sense of satisfaction if not elation.

Greater freedom of movement follows once the upright position has been achieved and the capacity to use hands and eyes increases. Concerted muscular effort produces its own reward in the form of greatly increased sensory stimulation, particularly in the visual field and in the form of tactile experience – which includes the development of skill in manipulating objects. Widening possibilities for all forms of exploration and manipulation provide a tremendous satisfaction and stimulate intellectual development. There is an increase in the whole range of possibilities for the child, accompanied by a strong sense of achievement which, in most cases, is amplified by the approving interaction with the parents during the prolonged growing up-years.

En route to this gradual acquisition of a sense of autonomy, power and feelings of importance, of equal importance is the incorporation of the downside, the inevitability of loss, disappointments and setbacks of various kinds. The toddler, having learned how to pull himself to the upright position, has the task of struggling with balance when standing or attempting to walk around. The bitter experience of losing balance, of falling and possibly being hurt in the process, counterbalances feelings of exhilaration. In the very early stages of learning to move around, the infant experiences the hardness of the real world and finds that it hurts when you fall and also when you run or walk into other solid objects.

The child learns all these things during the period of complete dependence on the parents. The way in which the parental role is woven into all this is vitally important. The nature of the mediation of the parents between the child and the world is crucial. It can either encourage a lively interest in what is happening all around, whilst providing necessary protection and boundaries and thus fostering a gradual movement towards independence, or it can damage or confuse the movement towards autonomy by lack of respect and protection for the dependent, vulnerable infant.

Some restrictions upon the wish for freedom of movement and exploration have to be accepted by the child. From the beginning, the whole gamut of possible emotions and sensations become interwoven; feelings about the satisfactions and disappointments of relationships become intertwined with those generated by the exhilaration and hurts resulting from the possibilities of movement. Feelings about the maintenance of the erect position and movements (active or passive) producing change in this position are frequently used as though they were equivalent to the feelings generated by the social experience of satisfaction or disappointment in relationships.

The transference of ideas about the attainment of the upright position for use in evaluating the experience of personal and social relationships

Feelings about the upright position, or loss of it, are transferred and used to describe the emotional aspects of relationships. Each individual is continually expending energy on growth, regeneration and on keeping upright and mobile. These growth processes depend on access to basic supplies. Becoming mobile after attaining the upright position is a core experience which affects us throughout life. We feel the loss of this latter state from time to time for various reasons: when we are ill, exhausted, when we fall or as we grow old and lose muscular and skeletal strength.

When learning to walk we frequently fall, and suffer many relatively minor hurts from which we soon recover. We quickly realize that falls are likely to be physically injurious and could even cause death, but we also soon learn that we have the capacity to heal and recover. The way in which these negatives and positives combine to form 'whole' experience is discussed later.

In parallel with this appreciation of the concrete reality of our world, our interactions with others produce satisfactions and/or disappointments. There appears to be emotional equivalence in the way we evaluate these two types of experience. Even interpersonal events are described using spatial terms to convey the emotional impact.

An awareness of the upright position dawns early in life. This awareness is revealed in play when the child experiments with objects by placing them in different positions and observing the characteristics of equilibrium in relation to the upright object.

Piaget (1954) reports on the observation of a one-year-old boy showing in his play 'an intentional search for the vertical position' (p.191). The child did this by placing a long box on its end so that it formed an upright. The same child, two months earlier, demonstrated an understanding of the relationship between an object and its support by placing one object on top of another. Piaget also reports that a girl aged fifteen months began stacking objects. Three months later, the same child succeeded in balancing six large blocks. The position of each was adjusted before letting go. She was able to foresee when the equilibrium would hold.

The awareness of uprights is often identified as being phallic in nature, which, of course, it sometimes is. But I think that the upright object embodies the state of equilibrium, which is something we have to maintain whilst moving around, though we rarely think about it. In a more general sense, the upright comes to represent an awareness of one's personal integrity and strength, plus the ability to initiate action and to be an individual in relation to others. The emphasis on the sexual connotation ignores this more basic meaning.

When uprights start appearing in a child's expressive material it is usually associated with growing self-awareness and confidence, just as the upward movement indicates increased awareness of feelings of power and autonomy. Images of a contrasting kind, such as broken-down objects, suggest the reverse, an awareness of a degree of injury to the budding psyche.

It is recorded that Queen Elizabeth the First remained standing for the last two weeks of her life because she thought that by doing so she would not die.

Primo Levi described how he felt after being ill and remaining in bed for a month: Though not fully recovered, he felt a strong urge to get up on his feet and put on his shoes. He had the clear impression that this would aid his recovery, even though he still felt weak, and had difficulty at first in standing .

After leaving the concentration camp he began to hope that, having survived endless years of upheaval, cruelty and massacres, he would see a world reorganized on 'upright, and 'just' foundations.

Trees are tall upright objects. For human beings, they possess valuable functions – some of which are real in the material sense, whilst others are of a symbolic nature. The shade provided by trees as well as the different possibilities for shelter from the elements are examples of the tangible benefits to be derived from trees. Trees are deified in some societies. One attribute which inspires admiration is the realization that a great tree has endured over time. Another reason for their capacity to inspire is that, by a process of identification, in looking at a tree we appreciate that with its upstanding bulk it represents a vast amount of energy used successfully to oppose the downward pull of gravity.

On the subject of trees, Jung (1964) says:

> We know that an ancient tree or plant represents symbolically the growth and development of the psychic life (as distinct from instinctual life, commonly symbolised by animals). (p.153)

We observe the repeated differentiation of branches and twigs as it spreads upwards and outwards and with this three dimensional pattern we can identify something of our own conscious thought processes.

Jung also said that 'since psychic growth cannot be brought about by conscious effort of will but happens involuntarily and naturally, it is in dreams frequently symbolized by the tree whose slow powerful growth fulfils a definite pattern.' (1964, p.161)

In using Lowenfeld techniques (as well as when observing ot her forms of play or looking at expressive material), attention needs to be paid to the relative positions of the objects and their movements (actual or implied) in the space provided. By the way in which the child does all these things, he is showing us something about the way in which he sees himself in relation to others. A characteristic pattern is produced. An exploration of such forms of self-expression leads to insight into the shape of the child's (or the adult's) inner world. Incidentally, it also indicates the nature of the individual's past and present relationships. This provides insight into the motivation of current behaviour. An individual's internal world is largely determined by the nature of his external world. One can be studied more meaningfully with reference to the other.

Examples from everyday speech of the transference of feelings, generated primarily in the physical world, to the sphere of interpersonal relationships

The perpendicular dimension includes both the ups and the downs in relation to the pull of gravity. The following examples are from everyday speech and they show how the emotional meaning of movement in the up/down direction is transferred to social experience. Possible examples are legion; the following examples are taken at random.

The adjective 'upstanding' is usually applied, not to a woman, but to a man (reflecting the fact that his status is usually higher) and might be prefixed by 'fine' or 'strong'; the qualities of individuality, integrity and confidence are implied. The term 'upright' focuses mainly on honesty, whilst the term 'bent' means the reverse. To 'stand up' for what you believe in suggests the courage to face opposition and possibly to risk some form of injury. To be 'upstanding' entails the risk of being knocked or pushed down. Such a person may or may not have his 'feet on the ground', which is a commonplace term for being in touch with reality. This state is in contrast with the condition of 'having your head in the clouds'. To feel as if you are 'on thin ice' conveys the idea of being in danger of being exposed in a bad light, whilst being 'in deep water' means that some kind of a struggle is going on to re-establish security of the self. Stevie Smith's (1964) poem, *Not waving, but drowning*, tells of someone who feels as if she is struggling in vain.

There are many different ways of being 'down' or of showing an interest in things that are down. Falling down, or being 'cast down' or 'cut down', all convey a loss of power, together with a sense of hurt or damage. The same applies to the terms 'underdog' and 'downtrodden', which also include a loss of status. To be 'put down' ranges from verbal humiliation to actual death.

The terms 'cast down' and 'cut down', as well as many of the other examples previously given, imply that the cause of the movement downward is attributed to some outside force. In other words, the subject was passive, that is the energy involved in the movement came from outside. Associated with the idea of energy is the fundamental notion of the source of supplies: necessary to generate energy.

The passive object, moved by an external force, usually ends up on the ground and so may be associated with mud, dirt, faeces or even with death. The idea of being abandoned or emotionally annihilated might be implied also. Not surprisingly, individuals who apply such images to themselves are feeling depressed, even if they may not be clinically depressed. Being 'in the pit' is a commonly heard expression meaning feeling extremely depressed.

All the above 'low' positions are being thought of negatively in relation to the upright. They are linked to 'bad experiences', very often related to feelings of deprivation, that is being cut off from the vital supplies. But there is one spatial idea involving lowness which goes against this generalization, feeling 'close to the earth' is understood to be a good, satisfying experience probably associated with continuity of loving care in infancy which is one of the most important human needs, and conveys such a fundamental feeling of being supported, of being at one with the universe and having close and easy access to the source of supplies. This feeling, no doubt, originates from early good experiences at the breast, before awareness of the up/down dimension, with its accretion of both positive and negative feelings, generated by close relationships, loomed into consciousness. I think it has something in common with the oceanic feeling.

Charles Rycroft (1968a) discusses the term 'oceanic feeling':

Phrase used by Romain Rolland in a letter to Freud to describe the mystical, cosmic emotion which (according to Rolland) is the true source of religious sentiments. Freud could not discover this feeling in himself. See Freud (1930), where he offers an interpretation of it, viz. that it is a regression, 'to an early phase of Ego-feeling', and revives the experience of the infant at the Breast before he has learnt to distinguish his ego from the external world. (p.105)

It seems that the oceanic feeling has its roots in those vital first stages of integration, described by Francis Tustin (1974) and discussed more fully in Chapter 3, concerned with the development of wholeness which is developed only through good satisfying early relationships.

Feelings associated with mud and dirt fall into two contradictory categories: positively, where the link may be with richness and value (witness the saying, 'where there's muck there's money') or negatively, where the link is with badness and a need for cleansing.

In the next paragraph are examples of feeling 'down' selected from clinical material. Some of the images appeared in 'Worlds'.

Examples from clinical material of the transference of feelings about the upright position – or the loss of it

At a fundamental level we know that, without a surface to support us physically, we fall, and would continue to fall until we came to a horizontal surface or support. And the term 'support' has nurturing connotations.

Sharrock (1968) quotes John Bunyan's description of his emotional collapse in his book *Grace Abounding* '…down fell I, as a bird that is shot from the top of a tree' (p.32).

In clinical material, feelings about the upright position – or the loss of it – are applied to unhappy relationships. The following examples involve the downward movement.

Sinking down

This is an idea which is often mentioned by children during damp sand play. One young boy described the softness of 'sinking sand' as 'horrible, it pulls you down, sucks you in'. This lack of solidity beneath the feet conveys powerful feelings of insecurity. Similar insecurity was being expressed by a boy in treatment who suddenly asked what was under the floorboards. One of his parents had already died and the other was seriously ill. In contrast, 'terra firma', with its solid physical support, conveys a feeling of security. Perhaps the commonly experienced dream of suddenly falling, which causes the dreamer to wake in a state of panic, is about fear of loss of the support, both physical and emotional, upon which we all depend. Rycroft's and Winnicott's ideas on vertigo, discussed below, are also relevant here.

Being sucked down

An eight-year-old boy was referred to the child guidance centre because he had learning difficulties. His teacher said that he gave her the impression of being 'low-spirited'. As he was running cars around in damp sand he began to talk about them being sucked down by snakes under the ground. The whole family was suffering from the fact that the father frequently behaved in an outrageous fashion, especially when he refused to take the medication for his manic-depressive illness.

Falling down, being knocked over or pushed down

Falling down is an image which appears frequently in a variety of forms. An image of a girl falling into a muddy pool was an incident in a complex World made by a ten-year-old girl called Christine. The image of falling into a muddy pool conveys a sense of powerlessness coupled with feeling dirty. Christine refused to go to school. During her therapy sessions she said that she had secrets that she would never reveal. She made it clear that she belonged to a family that was close-knit and loving. There was a suspicion on the part of the therapist of sexual abuse, derived from various suggestive clues. Christine is mentioned again on p.100 in discussion about distorted body image.

Christine had mentioned more than once that she had secrets. It is interesting to note the link between the suppression of information (secrets) and misuse of power. This occurs across the board, from abuse within the family to the harsh maintenance of power within the state. Information is itself a vital resource. Possessing strict control over information makes the exercise of power over others easier. Such control tends to be in the same hands that control other vital supplies.

Keith, a boy in his early teens, produced several versions of the experience of being 'down'. He once said that being tripped up had been the cause of all his problems; this had happened when he when he was playing football – a boy had fouled him. He had been kicked and pushed down. He conveyed the sense of humiliation. He also linked it to the way he felt when his parents complained about his behaviour and said that he was 'letting them down'.

Keith once drew a little man in profile who looked very much like his father. Keith was aged about eleven when first referred. He was anxious and obsessional. He had frightened his teacher by talking about suicide. He had been born to his mother when she was on the verge of the menopause. The pregnancy was said to have threatened her life. Her poor health was stressed. Keith was constantly worried about her condition. He was heavily dependent

Figure 1.1: Man with a chopper. Drawing by Keith aged about 10

'He chops down trees and cuts off bits that wave about and cut off light. He's about 80 years old and likes planting flowers as a hobby.'

upon both parents whilst harbouring anger towards them, which he was afraid to express. During a family interview, Keith's father became quite agitated thinking about the need to control children. He said that beatings at school had never done him any harm.

Hanging down

The Lowenfeld Mosaics have the potential to convey a wide range of spatial ideas. Keith, mentioned above, made a Mosaic very early in treatment. It was 'pendant' (Figure 1.2). This term applies to those arrangements of tiles which appear to be suspended from the further (upper) edge of the mosaic tray. This type of Mosaic is made by those who tend to be emotionally dependent on others, and this was the main feature of Keith's problem – an anxious preoccupation with his parents. To hang on is a primitive response, which can be observed in young babies, to maintain the vital physical link to the parent and to prevent falling. This instinctive need to hang on implies a basic awareness of the power of gravity.

Keith's own explanation of his chronic state of anxiety was in terms of having been forcibly moved downwards by being tripped or pushed. Hanging on, in a more positive sense, is discussed again later. Keith made a series of Mosaics during his three-and-a-half years of treatment, during which time he attended regularly once per week up to the time when he transferred to high

Figure 1.2: Pendant Mosaic made by Keith early in treatment

Figure 1.3: Cruciform Mosaic made by Keith towards the end of treatment
'The black has won. The red had to break up.'

school. One of his later Mosaics, in the form of a cross (Figure 1.3), is discussed later.

Lying down

Once again, in keeping with Keith's inability to stand up for himself, he described his feeling of fatigue when his father had left for work in the morning. He was then unable to get himself to school. He used to lie down as soon as his father had left the house.

Early in treatment Keith so clung to his parents that he was constantly preoccupied with them, unable to make the slightest criticism of them. Rycroft (1986b) describes this kind of inhibited individual in his book *Anxiety and Neurosis*. Later, Keith found an indirect way of crossing his mother. She took it as an insult when he put what she regarded as excessive amounts of tomato ketchup on the food that she had cooked. He would smile and continue the practice.

The invalid boy described in *The Secret Garden* by F. Hodgson Burnett (1975) spent all his time reclining in bed. From a position of physical weakness he tried to exert an omnipotent will over others. Later, his emotional and physical development was re-activated. These changes coincided with when he managed to get onto his feet and attempt to walk. By this time he was beginning to enter into positively reciprocal relationships with others. The maturing process was, by then, under way. In the psychological sense, the upright self, being fully involved with others, offers both strengths and weaknesses, the possibility of gains as well as losses, just as the toddler has to risk falling over in order to gain all the advantages of being able to stand up and move about.

Florence Nightingale is reputed to have wielded power and influence from her sick-bed. But this was only after she had already established herself as a force to be reckoned with. In her early adulthood she was a formidable character on the battlefield in the Crimean War. There she had saved lives by laying the foundation of modern nursing practice. Such was her reputation, later in life, that she was able to further her mission to put nursing onto a professional basis, using her influential contacts, working from her sick-bed.

Slipping down

W. de Kooning, the American painter, made a documentary film for television about the way in which he continued to paint after being diagnosed as suffering from Alzheimer's disease. He was pictured making a downward brush stroke, forming a downward slope intersected by a group of short curving lines (suggesting the curves of eyelids). As he worked, he said: 'It is being upright that bothers me... I'm slipping... I'm a slipping glimpser.'

Spiralling downward

In spatial language, this movement must surely represent the panic and fear around the idea of being abandoned, of being literally without support, emotionally bereft, in a state of great need. Jeffrey Dahmer (the serial killer) invented a game about trying to save yourself from spiralling downward which he played with a friend when they were boys. This game was probably an attempt to allay the anxiety he experienced through emotional insecurity. His biographer, Brian Masters (1993, p.30), reported the game and used this image of spiralling downward to represent the state of emotional destitution which pervaded the whole of Dahmer's life. His mother suffered from depression and was alcoholic. His father's professional life took up a great deal of his time and meant that the family moved house frequently (it is suggested that the one time Dahmer experienced a warm emotional relationship was when he was admitted to hospital as a small boy for an operation). I think that a prolonged state of emotional deprivation, particularly during the early years, constitutes severe abuse.

After carrying out several murders, Dahmer made a shrine, a horizontal shelf – that is a surface or support – where he stored relics taken from the bodies of his victims. This shrine marked the temporary arrest of his sense of falling, a brief respite from a chronic state of emotional isolation, of being totally without support. It seems to represent a fixed level, neither high nor low, an actual physical support to hold objects which were associated with positive emotions.

Vertigo

This quotation, from a paper on a case of vertigo by Rycroft (1953), is quoted by Winnicott as follows:

> Vertigo is a sensation which occurs when one's sense of equilibrium is threatened. To an adult it is a sensation which is usually, though by no means always, associated with the maintenance of the erect posture, and there is, therefore, a tendency to think of giddiness exclusively in terms of such relatively mature anxieties as the fear of falling over or the fear of heights and to forget that infants, long before they can stand, experience threats to their equilibrium and that some of their earliest activities such as grasping and clinging represents attempts to maintain the security of being supported by the mother. As the infant learns to crawl and later to walk, the supporting function of the mother is increasingly taken over by the ground; this must be one of the main reasons why the earth is unconsciously thought of as the mother and why neurotic disturbances of equilibrium can so frequently be traced back to conflicts about the dependence on the mother. (Winnicott 1958, p.97)

He continued:

> ...there is urgent need for us to hammer away at the discussion of the meaning of anxiety when the cause is failure in the technique of infant care, as for instance, failure in the technique of infant care, as for instance, failure to give the continuous live support that belongs to mothering. (pp.97–98)

Winnicott goes on to write:

> 'the states that are prevented by good infant care are all states that group naturally under the word mad, if they are found in an adult.' (p.98)

Being trapped in a tunnel underground

A depressed boy (Anthony), after a period of treatment, described how he had felt at the time of referral. He remembered that he had thought that life was like a long tunnel with birth at one end and death at the other. He had been referred for treatment because he refused to continue at school. He was about halfway through the 'O Level' course and had been expected to take about seven subjects. In school he was becoming extremely anxious in the presence of other boys. Though he was tall, well-built and quite good-looking, he had worries about his appearance. There were also anxieties about his sexuality.

A preoccupation with ideas involving mounds, tunnels and holes

A preoccupation with such ideas and with ins-and-outs is one way of expressing interest or concern about the functioning of the body. The severity of this kind of preoccupation can vary a great deal. It may merely be a need to be given permission to take a normal interest in sexual matters, as in the case of Dora. Or, with some children who are severely autistic, there is a fixation on a fragmented world of bodily sensations – a state graphically described in Francis Tustin's (1974) work on autism. Nurturing is characterized by lack of containment for the infant, which results in an in an inability to create the essential basic sense of wholeness of the self and of others.

Dora was 11 years old when she was referred for psychotherapy. Her attainment at school as well as her attendance were poor. A long list of physical symptoms, including tummy pains and constipation, came with the referral, plus a further symptom – 'alopecia of the eyelashes'. Her eyelashes had disappeared four years earlier. Dora's behaviour was like that of a much younger child, mainly as a result of her mother's dominating, over-protective behaviour. In her sessions Dora said very little, preferring to express herself either by drawing or by using the damp sand, which she sculpted, taking infinite pains, to make several Worlds made up of mounds, holes, pathways and tunnels, which were aesthetically pleasing.

These creations formed the basis for discussion, sometimes in terms of bodily functions, including procreation. Four months later her eyelashes re-appeared (I think that she had been pulling them out). Her behaviour in general became age-appropriate and she returned to school.

Dora made two patterns using the Lowenfeld Mosaics: one was produced at the beginning of treatment and the other shortly before she finished. The contrast in the configurations is striking and will be discussed later.

A very immature boy of six years, on his initial visit to the child guidance clinic, placed a doll on its back in the damp sand tray. He began plastering small

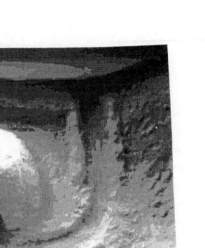

Figure 1.4: World in damp sand made by Dora

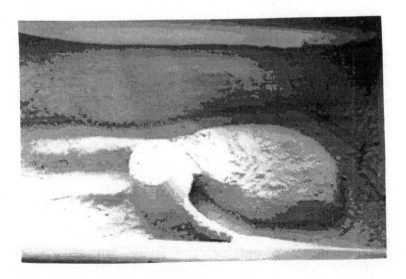

Figure 1.5: Second World in damp sand made by Dora

lumps of damp sand on top of it, starting at the mouth and going across to its bottom. He said that evil men were doing this to the doll. The boy was illegitimate, sharing a room with his mother in an old people's home where she was employed. Next door to this home was a dairy farm. When his mother went to visit her relatives many miles away, she left him behind. Her son was her secret, none of her relatives knew of his existence. On the nearby farm the herd of cows, looked after by the farmer, became a substitute for the missing extended family. I think that the way in which the doll was plastered with wet sand expressed something of the desperate hunger and anger, mixed with feelings of chronic depression, which he shared with his mother. I did not suspect that there was any other form of physical abuse.

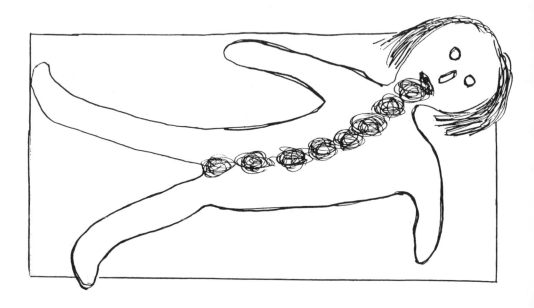

Figure 1.6: World in damp sand made by a six-year-old boy

An interest in ruins

A sense of desolation may be the resonance of the contemplation of a ruined castle. An eight-year-old boy called Peter painted such a picture. Peter was the elder son enmeshed in a very close but negative relationship with his mother, who had been deserted by her husband after a short but tempestuous marriage. She was a nurse, who gave the impression of being competitive in relation to other professionals. She expected Peter to perform well in school. He was considered to be an intelligent boy but his scholastic attainments were poor and it was difficult to get him to work in school. This was the main reason for his referral, apart from worry about 'silly' provocative behaviour. I think that the ruined castle represented the desolation felt by Peter, and probably the whole family, at the father's desertion. He had been a violent man and the parting had been acrimonious. (Constable painted 'Hadleigh Castle' after the death of his wife. It is a ruined castle – a powerful image of desolation and decay. It appears to have been painted from a high vantage point, giving a sense of remoteness from the earth. This is in marked contrast to his painting of 'The Cornfield', which shows a boy lying face-downward drinking from the stream, emphasizing both the support and the nurturing quality of closeness to the earth.)

By the time he was eight years old, Peter had become practised at thwarting the wishes of others, particularly if an attempt was being made to influence him in some way. The perverse reasoning seemed to be that the way to assert oneself was to deflect the efforts of others (the logic of the situation is similar to the way in which anorexic children, in a desperate bid to assert themselves, reject the food that is essential for their survival).

Figure 1.7: Drawing made on a blackboard on a wall by Peter

Peter illustrated his attitude to those in authority by drawing a picture of two figures (perhaps the therapist and his mother) falling off a cliff face whilst he stands triumphantly on the cliff top watching their descent. Most of Peter's energy was directed at undoing what others were attempting to do. In relation to treatment, there was collusion between mother and son, possibly unconscious, to make sure that no advances were made in his ability to progress and develop autonomy. She was possessive towards him, the eldest son, and competitive with other adults involved in his education. Peter's head teacher remarked on how uneasy she made him feel.

One day Peter drew a big bird at the bottom of a square hole, as if being looked down on from above. This drawing of a bird (which had had its wings clipped) is more fully described in the section about finding direction on page 99.

Feeling overwhelmed

Kevan, a deprived, vulnerable boy whose father had had a 'breakdown', painted a picture of a house lodged precariously between two hills near the sea, about to be overwhelmed by a tidal wave. He painted another picture about a month later showing that a change of mood had taken place. This painting, though in the form of a pair of pincers hanging down menacing a small boat, was of 'Mighty Me'.

Figure 1.8: 'Being overwhelmed' painted by Kevan aged 10 years

Figure 1.9: Second painting by Kevan painted almost a year later

Most of the above examples were gathered from the early stage of treatment when the child was remembering how it felt to be 'down', in an emotionally bereft state. The position of the self is low down, even below the surface – literally overwhelmed or submerged. For a good example of this kind of state, see James' first World on page 56. Another boy produced an image of people buried under a pile of rocks. External power is implied, movement having been exerted in a downward direction. For those on the receiving end of all this energy, feelings of helplessness and hopelessness coexist, at least temporarily.

Harry Guntrip (1968) discusses the occurrence of such introverted movements as are listed above. They are characteristic of individuals whose healthy development has been overlaid by fear, 'choked back and dammed in, in the schizoid personality' (p.92). The natural 'will to love and live' having been negated and replaced by withdrawal from life. Such passive or negative adaptations to life are discussed in Chapter 6.

The graveyard

An adolescent Asian girl was referred for treatment because she was out of school, spending a lot of time in bed. On her first visit to the clinic she arranged a small rectangular graveyard, behind a church, in the left-hand part of the damp sand tray. At the far side of the fenced-in tomb stones she placed an open gate, suggesting the possibility of an enticing 'way out'. Subsequently, she made more lively use of the World material. One of these was in the form of a maze (Figure 5.7, p.114).

Figure 1.10: A world in dry sand made by Kalyani aged 13 years

Hanging on

At a kind of intermediary position between being 'down' or 'up high', a woman described how she began to be able to cope with extreme mood swings by 'hanging on'. At extremes of emotion she either felt that she was 'in the pit' or 'up there'. When feeling low, she developed the capacity to 'hang on', remembering from past experiences that she could survive such states. Translating this 'hanging on' into concrete form, she used to hold a cross in the form of a hand or she would grasp a stone or a handkerchief. The 'hanging on' position is somewhere between being 'down' and 'high'. Using an object in this way appears to have something in common with Winnicott's 'transitional object'. It also suggests an awareness of the integrating process at work over time, where the act of 'holding on' helps the process of linking. Both despair and elation become softened by the awareness and memory of the other. The same woman said that she had begun to realize that there was no law which said that she must feel happy all of the time, so the ability to 'hang on' included a better appreciation of time and the possibility of linking different aspects together. This development is part of the maturational, integrating process bound up with the understanding of a system of secure, whole objects existing over time.

Looking back on the types of movement discussed so far, we started with the relatively passive movements where the object was subjected to outside forces – being sucked down, knocked down, tripped up, etc. 'Hanging on' and 'holding on', on the other hand, suggest the active maintaining of a position using energy from within – that is a movement towards autonomy.

Lowenfeld emphasized that in exploring an individual's inner world using various forms of expressive material, it is important to find out about the source of energy and the direction of movement. Also, the nature of the movement is important. Is it active or passive? During psychotherapy, in those cases where the predominant mood of early sessions was low, the turning point is sometimes marked by signs of movement in the opposite direction, as in the following examples.

Buoyant – that is, apt to float, rise up, keep or recover spirit

This is an adjective describing a relatively happy state of mind. The buoyancy of water is particularly interesting in relation to thinking about the emotional significance of maintaining the upright position with all its social connotations. When humans are immersed in water it has the effect of neutralizing the downward pull of gravity. Camus (1942) describes how the characters in his novel enjoy the sensuous experience of swimming in the sea which is so close to the towns. For them, swimming and floating in the sea is an escape from competitive pressures, and even from pestilence, present in the towns. Seamus Heaney (1991) in a poem *The Pulse*, described the experience of casting the line and standing on the bank of the river fishing. In a television programme discussing the poem he said that the activity gave him a feeling of 'beatitude', which, according to the Oxford dictionary, means a state of blessedness. Heaney said in the interview that whilst he was fishing he felt neither high nor low (perhaps something akin to feeling buoyant).

Sink or swim

At an intermediary stage during treatment, an eight-year-old girl named Nazia, spent several sessions testing the buoyancy of all the farm animals by placing them carefully, one at a time, in a sink full of water. Would they float or sink? Their fate was of the utmost interest to her as her own spirits had begun to rise. In the initial phase of treatment she had been suffering from her mother's depressed mood resulting from a sense of failure after giving birth to a girl baby when, culturally, a boy was most prized (fortunately, a boy was born later).

Gradually, over several sessions, Nazia's mood changed. Her spirits rose. Rather than being withdrawn, as she had been at the start of treatment when she used to sit with a coat over her head, she began to assert herself. As often happens, self-dislike was turned outwards and on one occasion her mother reported that she had slapped the face of a little girl relative. In the same vein, during one of her sessions she buried several small plastic chimpanzees in the damp sand, having given them her brother's name. It was his turn to be 'down'.

The action of slapping her small cousin was symptomatic of her own difficulty in accepting the vulnerable side of herself. She was bringing into the open her wish to be valued as a person in her own right. She tried to be all-powerful, as in the old rhyme 'I'm the king of the castle, get down, you dirty rascal!' At that time she drew pictures of hurt – limbs bleeding, for example. She gradually began to accept that these sad, hurt feelings were her own.

'The dive'

Some of the most valued tomb paintings at Paestum, Southern Italy (painted around 600 BC), are in the Temple of Neptune. One painting, called *The Dive*, shows a man diving into water, having jumped off a platform on the top of a high ladder-like structure on the right of the picture. It is not the athleticism of the dive which is the significance of the painting. The self-motivated descent symbolizes an idealistic movement away from materialism and individual power. The subsequent rise out of the water represents a movement towards embracing spiritual values.

Figure 1.11: A tomb painting at Paestum, Southern Italy, c.600 BC, in the temple of Neptune

In the Christian Baptism ceremony, where there is total immersion, the downward movement in water is associated with death and with washing dirt away. The subsequent movement upwards represents new life which is the religious sign of the resurrection. So, the ceremony embodies symbolism linking together life and death. Being able to link such opposing ideas in a creative way is an aspect of wholeness or greater maturity of personality.

Another of the tomb paintings asserts the importance of the cultural ideals of mutuality rather than competition. There are several paintings of figures reclining on benches. They are engaged in lively conversation or enjoying music together. Their individuality is symbolized by the facial profile, not the erect posture, which tends to be associated with the assertion of power. The fact that all are seated and seen in profile indicates the importance of each member contributing to group activities. The expression of relative individual power, within the group, is minimized (the existence of the slaves as an adjunct to the civilized life is left out of this system of ideas).

Spatial ideas incorporating the upward movement
Lifting up and being uplifted

This idea has already been touched on in relation to the infant's dependency and continuous need for support physically, but, most importantly, in the emotional, supportive sense.

Religious experience is often described as being uplifting – the good shepherd finds the lamb, lifts it up and carries it home. The infant is lifted up by the parent – is given food and comfort. At this stage parents are like gods, all-powerful. The infant has no autonomy, being subject to the mood of the parent.

Denis Nilsen, the serial killer, was interviewed for television and asked to talk about his crimes. He used the word 'conundrum' in relation to these questions. He recalled his feelings about being able to lift up and carry his dead victims. In particular, he remembered observing their dangling limbs. From what he said, it was as if he was enjoying the feeling of being all-powerful in relation to their inertness. Given what we now observe to be a tendency to reverse the situation in relation to the exercise of power, what does this suggest about his early relationships? To me, this urge to be all powerful implies that at an early stage in his life he had been overwhelmed by some experience, leaving him with the buried urge to 'turn the tables'. This drive to re-assert power after being 'put down' is a recurring theme in human interaction.

Those who have studied the personalities of a number of serial killers have found them to be isolated, fearful and threatened. Frequently, as children they experienced abuse of some kind. It appears to be a general tendency for those whose feelings of vulnerability have been severely provoked to turn the aggression outwards in identification with the aggressor. Further self-observations by Nilsen will be mentioned in a later part of this book. They throw light on his inner fragmentation and reveal his awareness of the perversion of his sense of direction.

Buried objects being dug up

This idea is readily expressed where 'World material' or sand trays are available. There are wide possibilities of meaning here. No automatic assumption should ever be made about the specific meaning of any clinical material. It is always necessary to ask the creator about the special significance of a particular object or form of expression. For example, an object such as a horse may be something ranging from gentle and friendly to powerful and frightening.

Sometimes, objects dug up represent the recovery of lost treasure. As such it is likely to be linked to a revival of a feeling of value about the self. It might linked to ideas about procreation – new life. I have sometimes found that the unearthing of buried objects has been used to represent the uncovering of secrets about past events or facts about family history, such as earlier separations and losses. For example, a mother may have had other children with whom contact has been lost. Working through such happenings within the therapeutic session produces insight and the possibility of further emotional growth.

An interest in things growing

Lack of feeling for growth is often symptomatic of retardation of the capacity to symbolize and is also characterized by a lack of three-dimensional structuring. If the inner world is still structured at this two-dimensional level there is a preoccupation with shapes and surfaces which sometimes overlap. At this two dimensional stage, there is no 'front and back' connection. Also, there can be no concept of internal space, which means that there is no possibility of there being any contents. Nor will internalized objects be capable themselves of being containers and of existing over time.

When an interest in growth and procreation appears, where previously it had been absent, it marks a movement towards the structuring of whole objects. The ability to conceive of the existence of whole three-dimensional objects makes it possible to think about the physical contents of the human body. As well as physical contents being conceptualized, it gradually becomes possible to deal with internal representations of experiences and feelings.

These representations form part of the internal structure. They may be stored, processed and assimilated. Memory and introspection allow access to these abstract, that is mental, contents of the body. These ideas will be discussed more fully in the next section about the conditions necessary for the forming of unity or wholeness.

Having achieved a three-dimensional state of understanding, children are likely to indicating their interest in procreation and nurturing. At this stage pictures are made of farms with animals such as pigs and piglets and with land being used to sow seeds or to grow crops. As mentioned earlier, closeness to the earth can represent 'good' feelings. Such pictures convey a sense of life and a satisfying feeling of well-being through being in touch with the source of supplies.

Climbing upward

An example of this idea is in the clinical material of a ten-year-old boy named Daniel. He drew and also wrote about himself attempting an arduous but determined struggle to climb a mountain (see Figure 1.12). The picture and story tell of hopeful striving towards love, recognition and power. But in the drawing, significantly, the top of the mountain is off the paper. This suggests a realization of the underlying hopelessness of his cause.

Daniel's mother tantalizingly held out the promise of love and approval whilst actually giving it to his older brother, in whom she saw all the virtue. Earlier in treatment Daniel had drawn a picture of a little man landing on a volcano with disastrous results! He said that the little man had thought that it was a safe place to land before it erupted. The family functioned around the mother's pathology. She was highly intelligent but was silent about her relationship with her own mother. Daniel was small for his age and she was keen to take him to hospital to look into the possibility of his being given growth hormones. At the same time, she made a practice of putting his breakfast on a high shelf so that he often went to school without breakfast and spent time scrounging for food. She then used to complain bitterly about this behaviour. It gave her further reason to be angry with him.

Apart from putting food out of his reach, she had other forms of physical abuse which stopped short of producing visible effects. She saw Daniel as a persecutory object (which was a mirror image of Daniel's experience of her) and admitted that she could not love him, although this attitude did not apply to her other children.

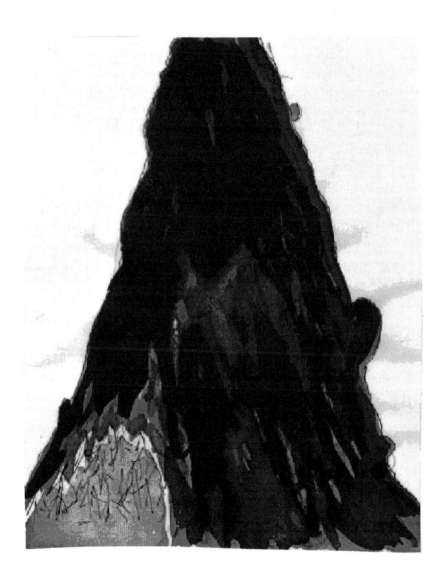

Figure 1.12: The Mountain, based on a painting by Daniel aged 10 years

This is the story that Daniel wrote alongside his drawing of the mountain:

> The Mountain Everest
>
> It is hard to climb the mountain Everest I've tried and tried it is impossible for you to do it I've slipped down twice it is not nice I'll try again and again I want to be famous and be famouser than ben(?) I nearly I nearly cryed I will soon do it Ill put my best mountain climbing suit on I will make it it is hard very hard.
>
> How hard it is how high it is ill do it. higher and higher I climb and still there is a lot more I want to jump to the floor I've tried and tried to climb the mountain Hillary did it Tenzing did it They took a long time to do it.
>
> Hillary is clever he must eat a lot yove got to take some food with you I will not have something to eat and drink climb the side facing New Zealand I will do it Ill try to do.

It is interesting that Daniel says he wants to jump to the floor, because, as Rycroft points out, the earth, or floor, at an early stage, is looked on as a secure position, rather like a substitute for being held by a parent.

Endlessly climbing upwards

The William Morris fabric designs were based on the idea of everlasting upward growth: patterns of stems, leaves and flowers endlessly climbing upward. It would be interesting to know how this one-directional idea about growth, used in his designs, linked to his personal life and his other idealistic ideas. Morris also spent time climbing mountains in Iceland.

An over-zealous attempt to climb upwards, socially as well as in other ways, is often explained in terms of compensation for a sense of maternal deprivation. The play *The Ascent of F6* by Auden and Isherwood explores this theme. Some might describe the everlasting upward movement as a defence against depression. Questions about the motivation of individuals who make determined efforts to achieve a high social status associated with the accumulation of great wealth sometimes brings forth suggestions that there is an overwhelming need to compensate for early deprivation. This leads on to an interest in the background of individuals who strive to become powerful leaders, perhaps tyrants.

Rockets poised to take off

Though representation of the phallus may be the obvious symbolism of a rocket, a more generalized meaning related to energy and the potential for self-assertion is, perhaps, more fundamental. The same might be said about the appearance in pictures (e.g. in Lowenfeld Worlds) of various perpendicular objects such as towers, posts, traffic signs, etc. Such manifestations are clearly in opposition to ideas of being down, broken down, etc. The up/down dimension represents the continuum of power: higher = more; lower = less. When 'sticking up' things occur, where there has been a spate of the reverse type of objects, this tends to support a view that there is growth in awareness of the growth of internal resources. It is not a coincidence that healthy self-assertion is called 'sticking up for yourself'.

Appearance of the 'little man'

The appearance of a 'little man', little more than a rudimentary upright object, at a certain stage in treatment suggests a strengthening of the sense of self or of self-awareness. Jung talks about the archetype of the 'little man' in dreams.

Figure 1.13: World in damp sand made by Janet aged 13 years
'A "little man" decorated with Christmas trees.'

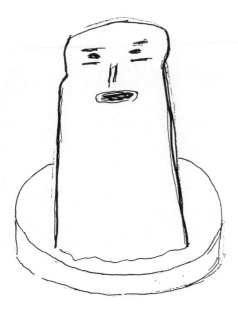

Figure 1.14: World in damp sand made by Kevan aged 11 years

'King-Kong – just a built statue. It was made in a round dish and on the right is a side view of it'.

Flying high in the sky

Birds flying may represent the human spirit and optimistic wishes for freedom and fulfilment. Victor Hugo had a strong identification with the underdog. In *Les Miserables* he described convicts as being 'eternal enviers of flies and birds'.

CHAPTER 2

James

A case study exploring difficulties in establishing the self as an individual amongst others

James' problem was very much concerned with power and an unhelpful pattern of having to control, or be under the control of, others. James was unable to enter into the normal give-and-take of life. Extreme anxiety about expressing his own feelings and fear about other people's intentions was stunting his development. The problem centred around power. It was as if, in terms of emotional development, he needed to emerge from his submerged state and assume the upright position.

James was almost eight years old when he was referred by school for lack of progress. The teachers described him as being a strange, vulnerable boy. At times in the past he had had aggressive outbursts, but now the situation was reversed. He was being attacked by other children. It was said that he sometimes actively provoked children to hurt him. As for formal learning in school, he had hardly made a start.

James needed a great deal of individual attention from the teacher. To help him settle, she often had to try and placate him by holding his hand and talking to him, as if he was a much younger child. James was exhibitionistic at times, in various ways, such as making a fuss when coming and going and making loud noises. He had exhibited his genitals once or twice. It was the suggestion to the parents that special educational provision might be needed for James which prompted mother to seek the help of the school psychological service. Father was almost never involved.

James was an only child. His mother was a teacher. Her manner was quiet and rather aloof. She said that James had been debilitated for the first four years of his life. This had been associated with high temperatures and ear ache. The normal developmental stages of infancy had been held up. He had needed speech therapy. He had been circumcised at the age of six years. Mother reported that, before the age of seven, he had so little energy that she often had to carry him home from school.

James' parents had little time for social workers and mother declined to become involved alongside the ongoing individual therapy for James. She was quite happy for James to have individual help but, at the same time, she protested that she really did not know what all the fuss was about. He was an 'angel' at home and she could 'manage' him perfectly well.

James' appearance was remarkable because it was so close to the image of the angelic cherub. His hair was golden brown in soft curls. His eyes were large and warm brown and he had long eyelashes. His complexion was a delicate creamy pink. In the very early sessions his manner was that of a sweet gentle child and his voice was babyish and placatory. At a later stage he showed himself capable of making extremely rapid switches in his emotional attitude. One day he arrived early and was asked to wait rather than going straight into the play room as he was about to do. This thwarting of his wish sent him into a state of white-faced fury. But when he realized that this was not making me change my mind, his attitude changed just as rapidly back to sweet placatory smiles. There was an element of disassociation in this behaviour, as there was later in his bouts of screaming. These started in the third week when he suddenly asked: 'Can I make a noise?' After being given a nod, he put his head back and uttered several piercing screams. These bouts of screaming occurred spontaneously and were not apparently connected to his play, nor did they appear to have much in the way of emotional content.

During early sessions he sought my reassurance by repeatedly asking: 'Are you my friend?' He would look into my face and ask: 'If you are my friend, why don't you smile at me?' He seemed to need reassurance from this powerful authority figure – the therapist. This need to look into 'mother's' face is characteristic of early infancy. His teacher remarked on something similar in his behaviour at school. He always had to seek her out to say 'goodbye' at the end of the school day, as if to reassure himself that they were still on good terms. His behaviour suggested a high level of anxiety and raised questions about his treatment at home. Little was known about the dynamics within the family. James' father was rarely seen at school and he never visited the clinic.

It was James' unease in his relationships with those he saw in positions of authority over him which was one of the main characteristics of his behaviour in the early stages of treatment. He was hungry and demanding in his wish for instant attention, with lots of smiles and reassurance. As part of his anxiety in relation to those he saw as powerful figures, he at times sought permission to do certain things, as he had done over the urge to scream. This came to a climax after several months of treatment.

James' mother encouraged imaginative self-expression and his father had artistic interests. These facts may partly explain why James so readily took to using the Lowenfeld World material. His concentration on creating a World carried him through most sessions. He worked systematically and appeared to know exactly the kind of picture he was trying to achieve. The development of his language accompanied the progress in his spatial ideas.

In the first few sessions James spent a lot of time examining the wild animals. His speech was slow but clear. He used a 'singsong' intonation which seemed strange for an eight-year-old boy. He would say 'Here's a crocodile!' and, a few seconds later, 'Here's another crocodile!' All the wild animals were taken out of the drawer one at a time. They were classified as 'damaged' (if a piece was broken off) or 'not damaged'.

The damaged animals were immediately discarded. He noticed that the penguin had a foot missing. It was pronounced dead and discarded. He said that he did not mind if the other children played with the damaged toys but only the whole animals were any use to him. He called them 'my animals' and said that he alone should be allowed to use them.

Six Worlds, all clearly defined and well organized, have been selected from the series he made during his year of therapy. The general pattern of each World tended to be carried on from one week to the next, as if he was gradually working something out. Such a high level of continuity is, I think, fairly unusual. Each World reproduced here has similarities with others in the series, which illustrates the way in which his ideas evolved during the year he was in treatment.

My animals (29th June 1980)

This World was made in James' sixth session. It gave a graphic picture of his submerged state, hanging on to his mother in a twilight world.

He said that the dinosaurs belonged to him but were far too dangerous to be allowed near the other animals – they would eat them up! They were all put in a large tin with the lid pressed down hard. James said very little during this sorting out process, apart from his infantile way of naming each animal. He also made it clear that words from me were not welcome. He seemed to experience them as intrusions into his private world.

First, he built up the damp sand on the left hand side of the tray to form a sloping bank. All the wild animals – elephants, giraffes, rhinos, hippos, monkeys and a lion – were taken one at a time and pressed down hard into the damp sand. In front of the lion was placed his 'two meats' – two pieces of meat skewered on poles, as seen in the zoo to feed to the lions. The significance of this was expressed later. With the left-hand side of the tray filled with the

Figure 2.1: World in damp sand made by James on 29 June 1980

'The turtle in its shell and the octopus with its suckers for hanging on are both submerged in a twilight world.'

sloping bank crowded with animals, the right-hand side was flooded with water. On the edge of the water, in the middle of the tray, two animals, the turtle and the octopus, slithered around close together. From time to time the turtle made a hole to hide in. The octopus scurried out of the water but was soon back close to the turtle. They circled around each other in the shallow water. Nothing else happened. James pointed out that the octopus had suckers for 'hanging on'. Later, two 'very dangerous' crocodiles were placed well away on the right.

The submerged self

All the action centred on two central objects: the turtle in its shell and the octopus with its suckers. They circled round each other, submerged in a kind of twilight world. James was stuck at an early infantile stage well summed up by the picture of a rather desperate 'hanging on' whilst being submerged in water or hiding in a hole. A kind of symbiotic attachment held the turtle and the octopus together, giving some impression of the nature of relationships within the family.

Other energy sources were split off: dinosaurs were trapped into a tin, wild animals immobilized by having their feet embedded in the sand and, some distance away, was the threatening presence of the hungry crocodiles.

Apart from the slithering around of the two animals under water, it was a very static picture containing plenty of suppression and control – indicated by the downward pressure which James used to put the animals in their place. The World he so carefully set out illuminated the nature of his enmeshed relationship to his mother. Just how the father fitted into the triangle was not known.

All the sand was put into a bank on the right. Indians and Daleks confronted each other on the bank. A hole was made in the bank. Real water was added on the left which formed violent waves breaking up the bank.

This was the conclusion of this world. The whole was enlarged and all the objects were stuffed into the hole and churned up.

The Daleks (21st September 1980)

This World was made in James' thirteenth treatment session (he had not attended during the school summer holidays).

A sloping bank was formed on the right-hand side of the damp sand tray. A group of cowboys, a totem pole and three tents were put on the bank. Water was poured in on the left. Then the Daleks arrived, repeatedly shouting 'Exterminate!' They shot people with their projecting arms. The two groups

Figure 2.2: World in damp sand made by James on 21 September 1980

Figure 2.3: The same World in damp sand made by James on 21 September 1980

fought but neither side emerged victorious. James then made a tunnel in the bank. Water was made to wash up into the bank. The attacking waves became wilder and caused the hole to enlarge and the bank began to disintegrate. All the objects were stuffed into the hole and eventually the whole lot was churned up together.

Compared with the earlier World, the static quality has been replaced by powerful movement involving water. The various elements interacted aggressively. The tunnel and the penetrating water, not to mention the totem pole and other phallic elements, may be interpreted as expressions of sexual/bodily enquiry.

'My Land' (11th February 1981)

This World was made about nine months from the start of treatment. It was James' 28th session.

All the damp sand was formed into one large central mound which he called 'My Land'. By this time James liked to enlist my help in making his Worlds, provided I was careful to follow a definite lead from him. The sides of the mound were made very steep – as near to vertical as possible. This is something which Lowenfeld pointed out: the fact that a mound usually followed in the same position where previously there had been a hole or a hollowed out area. Heaping the sand up and making the sides very steep tended to make the mound unstable and James was anxious to keep the mound all in one piece. In these spatial terms, James was objectifying his difficulty. He needed to assert his individuality and, at the same time, to defer to his parents.

He asked me to help him make a Union Jack flag. When this was done he stuck it in the top of the mound. There were no Daleks in this World as they had been got rid of in the previous session. The mound was called 'My Land' because it was only for him and his friends to share. His friends were the following animals: elephants, giraffes, monkeys and lions – including one lion with his 'two meats'. There was also the little turtle who earlier hid in holes and a rhino with a powerful horn. As usual, the animals had their feet deeply embedded in the sand – but as this was on the steep sides of the mound, their position was very insecure.

Two things now began to increase the instability of the mound, together with that of the animals hanging onto its sides: the rhino began to ram his horn into the base of the mound with a great deal of energy and lots of water was poured in round the base of the mound. The ramming of the horn and the swishing of the water brought about the total disintegration of 'My Land'.

Figure 2.4: World in damp sand made by James on 11 February 1981

James embedded all his animals on a very high mound. A Union Jack was stuck in the top.

This World was, at first, centralized and clearly less fragmented than earlier worlds. The steep-sided mound represented a powerful movement upwards in that all the sand was drawn up centrally where, in a previous World, it had been hollowed out to make the pool for the enmeshed turtle and octopus.

The mound, with its complement of animals, represented various aspects of James' complex emotional life, which was still excessively bound up with his relationship with his parents. He still clung to them anxiously and was unable to make relationships with his peers. The choice of a Union Jack flag, in particular, suggests that the mound represents the triangular nature of the tight bonds within his family which were hampering his development as an individual.

'My Land' – second version (28th February 1981)

This World was made the week after the emotional crisis (described later) had erupted on the pretext of where James was to place his Spiderman doll. James still looked rather subdued. The previous week's events were referred to in terms of his wish for the therapist to be a good kind mother who always said 'Yes' to her baby, but this was not possible. The following two Worlds made in damp sand were clearly on the theme of breasts – the good followed by the bad.

Good breasts were made first. In damp sand he made a large mound with several small round mounds on top. He caressed these lovingly for some time. Then the mound underwent a dramatic change. It turned into a volcano. Whilst this change was taking place, he screamed several times. To make the volcano, the centre of the large mound was hollowed out and water was put inside – representing 'hot lava'. James was able to link this to his distress of the last session. He said that he had felt as if he was bursting with all the hotness inside (this 'hotness inside' almost certainly links to a much earlier symptom during infancy reported in his social history. The debilitation which he suffered from in his early years was associated with high temperatures and ear ache. No satisfactory explanation was ever given for this condition). Talking about the lava and the 'hotness inside', he said: 'it can turn you to stone'. During the eruption of the volcano, as well as emitting screams, he used swear words such as 'shit' and 'fucking bastard' in a disassociated manner.

This World shows that there is the beginning of an interest in insides and all that this implies. It was becoming more natural to acknowledge feelings and to talk about them.

Figure 2.5: World in damp sand made by James on 28 February 1981

This represents rounded breast-like mounds.

Figure 2.6: World in damp sand continued by James on 28 February 1981

This shows how the breast-like mounds were transformed after a pond had been put in the centre. The breasts turned into a volcano and lava poured out.

Looking for enemies (8th March 1981)

This World was made in the 35th session. James started by making a large, high mound containing all the damp sand scraped up and patted together. Two giraffes were pressed down hard in the top. They were 'looking for enemies' – looking into the far distance. This represented his need for vigilance, resulting partly from his excessive anxiety about how to relate safely to other people and also about how to deal with his own emotions. The mound was surrounded by water.

The story which unfolded centred on the baby elephant. James explained that the Daleks were supposed to be looking after the baby elephant but all kinds of unpleasant things kept happening to him. The wild animals did all kinds of nasty things to him and he was afraid that his trunk would be pulled off. The lion was present, as usual, with his 'two meats', which were on two sticks in front of him. These 'meats' represented breasts. James confirmed this and said that when he was punished by being sent upstairs, he had the idea of detaching mother's breasts and taking them up to his room. As the animals were positioned on the mound, the significance of the various animals was discussed.

Was the turtle, in the way he always needed a hole to hide in when he was frightened, like someone who clung to mother for protection? In response to this question, James showed how the Daleks dragged the turtle out of a hole and threw him on one side! The rhino with his thrusting horn represented phallic preoccupations. The Daleks represented his dominant urge for control over everyone, including himself.

Towards the end of the session, the rhino again used his horn to break up the mound. This time, instead of ending with churned-up confusion, James heaped up sand in the near right-hand corner, calling it 'new land'. He transferred all his animals to this new 'safe' area.

This World again shows an increased capacity to conceptualize and focus on feelings that are very important to him. The way in which all the damp sand was gathered together and formed into one large mound seems to represent awareness of powerful resources which, at the same time, were precariously based. The break-up at the end made way for re-structuring.

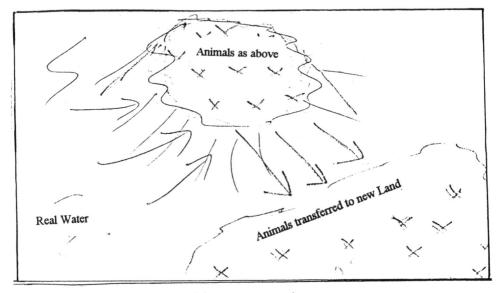

Figure 2.7: World in damp sand made by James on 8 March 1981

Two tall giraffes are on the top of the mound 'looking for enemies'. The rhinoceros was already attacking the bottom of the mound.

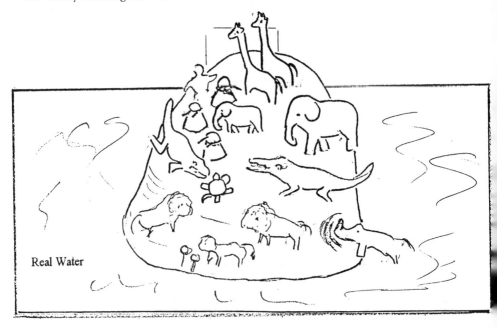

Figure 2.8: World in damp sand continued by James on 8 March 1981

This shows how the World developed when water surrounding it produced violent waves destroying the mound. The animals were transferred to new land on the right of the tray.

The Daleks and the intruders (13th June 1981)

This World was made about one year after the first one of the series. James gave a definition of 'an intruder'. He said that it is 'someone who comes when you don't want them to'. This might well apply to his attitude to his own feelings, as suggested by Rycroft. But another interpretation emerged during the making of the World.

The World, using damp sand, was divided down the middle. All the sand was banked up on the left so that it sloped to the centre of the tray. Trees were dotted around in the sand and four Daleks were grouped under the trees. The right-hand side of the tray was empty until three male figures, the intruders, were introduced.

James told the story. The intruders had landed in the Daleks' land. They had not known, prior to landing, that there were Daleks in the area. The Daleks found the intruders. James spoke for the Daleks in their monotonous, metallic voice:

'Why do you come here? Why don't you leave us alone?'

'There are only Daleks and trees and sand here!'

'Why don't you leave us alone?'

'You will go away! Why don't you walk around and look at the trees?'

'We can enjoy ourselves.' 'You are bothering us!'

'We don't want to be disturbed!'

The intruders said 'No!' and refused to go away.

The Daleks continued to drone on, trying to drive them away.

'If you go away, we can have fun and play on our own!'

'Why don't you go away?'

'We will get rid of you!'

'You can't pick the apples. They belong to us!'

'If you are hungry, you can damn well bloody starve!'

At one point, when the Daleks were trying to send the intruders away, I made the comment that the Daleks sounded rather like grown-ups talking to a very young child; it sounded as though the child was the intruder and the grown-ups loved one another. James replied quickly, 'Yes but they do love the baby!'

Towards the end of the session the intruders made holes in the bank near the trees, put water in the holes and pushed the Daleks inside.

Figure 2.9: World in damp sand made by James on 13 June 1981

'The Daleks and the intruders'. This world was made about one year after the first in the series.

Discussion about the progress during James' year in treatment

The retarded state of James' emotional and intellectual development seemed to result largely from the excessive anxiety which he experienced in relating to everyone. This applied to relationships within his peer group as well as to those in authority. Ordinary self-assertive and aggressive impulses had been largely bottled up, as had wishes to have some control.

The anxious way in which he had to monitor my attitude towards him, particularly in the earlier sessions, showed fear in the transference. This expression of his inability to relate to others with a degree of confidence came to a climax in a later session.

The use of the transference to provide a fresh learning situation is undoubtedly a tool to facilitate change, but it is not the only means. During play the creative and emotional effort of objectifying the inner world, using real objects (which, in turn, reflects the nature of real relationships past and present) in the insightful presence of a therapist, also facilitates the growth process.

Several months into treatment, in September 1980, James was beginning to express himself verbally with more freedom. He remembered how he had tried to make himself into a Dalek by getting inside a cardboard box. He had poked out a piece of water pipe as one of the projecting arms used to exterminate other beings. He explained how the Daleks had two projecting arms, one to expel water and the other smoke. The Daleks appeared in many Worlds. They seemed to represent his internalization of the authoritarian side of his parents, harsh and metallic.

Without any prompting from me, he told me that he did not like the idea of other children being in the therapy room and using the toys. He discussed the difficulties he was having in mixing with the other children at school, adding, in a matter of fact way, that he felt like punching their teeth in.

In February 1981, when he was setting up a mound full of 'my animals', he said that with his bionic eye he could see Daleks and dinosaurs in the distance. This prediction was soon confirmed. It centred on problems about the form of authority and control between the two of us in the play room. These were worked on in the transference and came in the form of a highly emotional confrontation with me as his therapist.

One day James brought his Spiderman doll to the session. He asked if he could put this doll on the top of a large wooden box. I told him that he was allowed to put his doll wherever he chose. This was not the reply that he wanted. He repeated the question, demanding the reply 'Yes'.

Several times the question and answer were repeated but he would not accept the open-ended reply. He simply wanted me to say 'Yes'. This demand was insistent but it was not met, because to do so would have meant colluding with his idea that I was in control of his actions, lessening his autonomy. In his effort to extract the response he wanted, he became extremely worked up. He lay on his back on the floor, becoming very red in the face, still pleading for the word 'Yes'.

He chose to ignore the fact that he was being offered a wider choice of action, including putting the doll on the box. The distress experienced by James was palpable. Having to withstand his pleading made me feel very uncomfortable indeed. I tried to put his feelings and my feelings into words. But there was a paradox at the heart of this highly charged situation: in trying to make me to say 'Yes', he was attempting to force me to control him.

If I had complied with his demand I would have been perpetuating his need to submit to authority rather than to decide something for himself. James finally resolved the situation in his own way. After lying on the floor frantically pleading for several minutes, he suddenly got to his feet and said that he would take the doll to his mother. He went quickly alone to the waiting-room and put the doll in his mother's bag. He came straight back, told me what he had done with the doll and continued the session still showing the effects of the emotional upheaval.

Charles Rycroft (1968b) describes the way in which submission and control each appear intermittently in those who exhibit this kind of hysterical, submissive defence. He writes:

> Habitual adoption of the hysterical, submissive defence does not abolish aggression and self assertion, but sends it underground and in persons who use this defence extensively, 'the return of the repressed' manifests itself in devious forms. Either the worm will turn intermittently, leading to short-lived ineffective attacks of 'hysterical' rage, or the submissive role will itself be exploited in a way calculated to control others by making them feel guilty, or the conviction of being a defeated person will be used to justify underhand methods of manipulating others. (p.89)

James' history of excessive fatigue, reported by his mother, is symptomatic of this type of neurosis. Rycroft explains it in terms of the expenditure of so much energy maintaining his internal *status quo* by means of inhibition.

Rycroft explores the characteristic behaviour of patients suffering from anxiety associated with uncertainty about the source of control in relationships. He says that increasing self-understanding is an active way of getting on top of personal problems. But, if in psychotherapy the patient is mainly seeking protection and guidance from his therapist, he compounds the original neurosis by adding to it the neurotic response of submission to authority. I take this to mean that the therapist needs to refuse the 'authority' role and to provide a situation which shifts the balance of power in favour of the patient.

Rycroft goes on to discuss the compulsion to control everyone and everything, this being a characteristic of obsessional neurosis:

> Whereas healthy persons engage in spontaneous relationships in which they allow free interplay of emotions between themselves and others, expressing and receiving affection and anger without anxiety, obsessional characters attempt to control their emotions and to pin down both themselves and others in predetermined positions and attitudes. In this way they hope to avoid anxiety by eliminating the unpredictable element in human relationships. (1968)

When the obsessional demand for control lessens, insecurity – mentioned during the creation of World three – makes its appearance. The concern about whether or not the mound would hold together was created in this World and became the focus of his anxiety. If the unstable mound symbolized the way in which he was embedded in his family, the instability itself could be viewed as a movement towards healthy conflict – necessary if he was ever to develop emotionally by separating himself off from his parents. James was still clinging to the security of his dependent relationship on them but, at the same time, there were stirrings of a contrary nature – the need to assert his individuality – represented earlier by the destructive water and the rhino. In other words, they, perhaps, represented the wish to break away from the restricting parental bonds. Throughout the development towards adulthood and separation from parents there is the gradual widening of boundaries and a relinquishing of control and authority on the part of the parents.

It is interesting that Rycroft mentions the fact that the obsessional personality feels 'antagonism towards emotions as such, and feelings come to be regarded as intruders which disturb the orderliness of the world of which the obsessional has made himself the master.' (1968b, p.77). In the sixth World made by James, intruders made their appearance. James' treatment came to an end soon after this session as the family moved away. Mother had by this time reported changes in his behaviour. He had started taking part in adult conversations. Both parents had noticed this and were pleased. Reading and other school work was improving but James was still reporting that other children were bullying him. There was no doubt that treatment needed to continue.

CHAPTER 3

The development of wholeness

Degree of wholeness varies – according to the level of integration

Throughout our lives we are active in a process of adaptation, with the general aim of satisfying our needs and wishes. This is effective if we have attained a degree of wholeness in the way we structure our world. This level of integration only comes about if a similar level of integrity already exists within the environment itself.

For the individual, the terms 'wholeness' and 'integration' are spatial ideas used to describe a state of emotional maturity, which, at its most effective, moderates opposing feelings of omnipotence and weakness by relating them together. This aspect of development, which links together the extremes of strength and weakness, is infinitely more complex than is the awareness of the up/down axis.

Given the complete dependency of the human infant, a striving for mastery, developing in tandem with a strong sense of interdependency, is a healthy state of affairs. A vital awareness of the self (gradually represented internally by a sense of wholeness and uprightness) develops in relation to an appreciation of others. When this happens, the chance of individual survival is increased because internal energies can be effectively organized within the constraints of the particular social setting. A legitimate sense of direction is then possible. This development is more likely to be achieved by individuals born into a social setting which provides both challenges and reasonable access to resources.

Wholeness, as a tendency, is relative – according to the degree of complexity of understanding of the self in relation to the outside world. An individual can only become whole to the extent, and in the manner, that his family and culture allows.

Developing wholeness in the initial stage of life

For the infant, the basis for a useful system of (whole) ideas develops through an effective and mutually satisfying give and take, primarily with the mother. This produces a reasonably firm sense of self, which, to a large extent, reflects the degree of wholeness within the parents. A well-developed state of wholeness makes possible autonomy and a sense of direction, coupled with the dawning of self-awareness or self-consciousness. Self-recognition can only come about when a sense of permanence and continuity over time has been achieved. Other spatial ideas, used to characterize the state of integration of unity as an individual, are being 'centred' and having 'inner balance'.

From flickering sensations, self-awareness gradually strengthens through their integration. The infant develops an understanding of himself and others, each occupying a place in the scheme of things. Social understanding which emerges is inextricably tied up with such physical developments as the ability to hold the head erect, to sit up and look around and, eventually, to stand up and walk. Managing to maintain a position against the downward pull of gravity fosters the sense of individual power.

Gradually, over years, children establish themselves with a degree of independence. First, there is the dependency on the active mediation of parents. Their sensitivity during the nurturing process is vital. The infant's needs may then be met while, at the same time, maintaining protection and control. A system of whole objects is created. At the heart of this three-dimensional state, which includes constancy of shape developed through sequencing of sensory data over time, is a stable vantage point lodged within the upright position. This stable reference point, which enables the individual to make some kind of sense of their world, is established through mutually satisfying relationships. Basic wholeness becomes established.

Some children become enmeshed in a relationship with parents who, for personal reasons, are unable to respect the child's integrity. This means that the balance of power remains with the adult. Parents may be unable to perceive the infant as an separate entity, particularly if their own ego is weak. They may use the immature individual to supply their own inappropriate emotional needs. In these cases the emotional immaturity of the parents has a destructive effect.

It is clear that children brought up in inadequate or perverse nurturing situations are going to have the utmost difficulty in establishing themselves as individuals. The self, which is partly represented by the perpendicular, has not been able to stabilize itself against a backdrop which is both unreliable and threatening. This kind of environment tends to disrupt the logic of thought and produce erratic behaviour. 'Our unity as individuals is not something given. It is a continuous lifelong project, an effort constantly undertaken in the face of endlessly disintegrating forces.' (Midgley 1994, p.23).

At all levels of the integrating process, social interdependency is vital:

> No creature has evolved as a solitary mathematician. And even if human beings had for some reason wished to withdraw into a more solitary way of life, they could not possibly have done so, because the special development which raised their level of intelligence demanded of them ever more not less, co-operation, affection, mutual help and interdependence. (Midgley 1994, p.119)

Moral concepts are present in all human interaction. One way of defining wholeness is in terms of behaviour and the degree to which a balance is struck between personal needs and those of others. Implicit in this definition is the place of moral ideas in all human interaction.

In discussing the sources and meaning of morals, Mary Midgley is very critical of traditional ideas which contrasted thought with feeling. She points out that the cognitive and emotional aspects of the ability to feel sympathy, for example, are conceptually inseparable. She defines morality in terms of the shared solutions to the unavoidable fact of conflict in social life. Well developed emotional and cognitive components of the ability to feel sympathy are rooted in an individual's membership of a reasonably integrated family/society which values such attributes.

Psychotherapists work with people who have had to contend with a preponderance of adverse conditions, usually social, which, in various ways, overwhelmed the sense of self which was not strong enough to cope. In biological terms, these setbacks were connected with difficulties experienced in gaining access to the necessary resources. At an early stage of development discontinuity and pain make adaptation to reality unbearably difficult. This experience hampers the appreciation of an essential unity which is normally acquired at the sensori-motor level. Generically similar concepts then remain separate because of the extreme difference between associated affective states. The result is that an appreciation of wholeness does not develop. In treatment the aim is to reactivate the integrating process.

A regular supply of material/emotional support is necessary to build up the infant's perception of regularities, so creating an internal world characterized by 'wholeness'. Such nurturing conditions could be said to provide 'containment', which in itself is a form of wholeness. This interlocking of the inner world with the outer world will be explored more fully later.

A biological explanation for the development of intelligence, that is, the capacity to think, is given by Piaget (1947). He describes the nature of psychic growth, which he calls intelligence, as resulting from a striving to re-establish equilibrium, which is a process which continues throughout life. Intelligence directs behaviour to satisfy a need. The structuring of intelligence (cognition) is built up during the individual's efforts at adaptation, or re-adaptation, in response to the experience of needs. The affective side of this process is seen in terms of valuation or energy.

The capacity to think should not be thought of as a faculty but as something which develops in the process of interaction with the environment. Piaget underlines the fact that there is continuity between the higher forms of thought and the whole mass of earlier types of cognitive and motor adaptation. This brings us back to one general theme of this work, i.e. the fact that spatial thinking and verbal (linear) thinking are inextricably linked. Both have an emotional dimension.

Through exploratory behaviour, the child develops his perception of the world. This exploration is both visually and physically manipulative. When a young baby throws objects out of his pram and watches them find a surface, one of the things he is exploring is gravity. He also, at the same time, learns about social relationships by experiencing how his behaviour is responded to by other people. When objects are returned to him, the idea that objects exist over time is encouraged, as is his attachment to others.

Piaget (1954) describes how the infant spends time holding objects, moving them around whilst observing the visual transformations:

> ...during this stage the child begins to impart to objects movements of translation, horizontal and in depth, in order to study the latter. Just as he hides objects in order to find them again, moves them away from him and towards him in order to examine their apparent transformations, so also does he displace them simply to study their movement. (p.166)

This activity (observed in the case study of Jackie and reported on p.88) contributes to visual sequencing, which eventually forms an integrated structure, that is, object constancy. Such 'perceptual constancy' is, in fact, comparable at the sensori-motor level with the various ideas of 'conservation' which characterize the first conquests of intelligence (conservation of wholes, substance, weight, volume, etc). Given that Piaget understands that intelligence is not a faculty but something which develops through active engagement in social events, it follows that he should discuss the kind of social environment which would support healthy cognitive/emotional development. He states that, for the child, the social environment is not distinct from the physical environment. Piaget talks about the need for a social background of co-operation in order for good development to occur. In other words, a basic level of social integration is a necessary condition for the fostering of individual integration:

> ...in order to teach others to reason logically it is indispensable that there should be established between them and oneself those simultaneous relationships of differentiation and reciprocity which characterise the co-ordination of viewpoints. (1947, p.162)

> In fact, it is precisely by a constant interchange of thought with others that we are able to decentralise ourselves in this way to co-ordinate internal relations deriving from different viewpoints. (1947, p.165)

Logic can only be constructed from wholes and from this point of view serialization, that is, the linking of a series of different perceptions of the same object to form a whole object, is the only reality (Piaget 1947). This understanding is dependent upon the wholeness of perceptions built up during the first two or three years of life. Substance and space should be considered simultaneously. During the elaboration of the inner world, emotional and intellectual aspects emerge as distinct, though, in fact, they are interdependent. Gradually, through the continuity of a 'good-enough' nurturing experience, the baby arrives at the notion of constancy of objects. This makes possible the rudimentary understanding of space and time, which is the basis of logical thought and co-operative behaviour.

In a reasonably good nurturing environment the infant systematically builds up from serialized sense impressions the constancy of solid objects. Concepts of causality and time flow naturally out of the structuring of the three-dimensional world. The focus of such satisfactory development is the way in which the mother acts as a mediator with reality for the child.

Winnicott (1958) describes the mother's role as follows:

> It is especially at the start that mothers are vitally important, and it is indeed a mother's job to protect her infant from complications that cannot yet be understood by the infant, and to go on steadily providing the simplified bit of the world which the infant, through her, comes to know. Only on such a foundation can objectivity or a scientific attitude be built. All failure in objectivity at whatever date relates to failure in primitive emotional development. Only on the basis of monotony can a mother profitably add richness. (p.153)

> ...with good-enough technique the centre of gravity of being in the environment-individual set-up can afford to lodge in the centre, in the kernel rather than the shell. The human being now developing an entity from the centre can become localised in the baby's body and so can begin to

create an external world at the same time as acquiring a limiting membrane and an inside. (p.99)

Through the mother's integrity, the baby is enabled to develop his own. Francis Tustin (1972) describes this positive process:

The inner sense of 'linking' provided by satisfying experiences of encircling the nipple in the mouth, of being encircled in the mother's arms, and of being held within the ambience of the mother's caring attention seems to be a vital first step from which integration can begin to take place. This is integration of various parts of the personality, and also integration of the emergent self into a situation where other 'wills' exist apart from his own. If this sense of primal linking is lacking, processes exclusively centred on the child's own body compensate for the lack… (p.59)

Parental nurture provides facilitating conditions,

…but such nurture may be grossly lacking. Or, and this may be a far more common cause, the reception of nurture may be severely blocked or confused due to some variety of factors. Without, or unable to make use of nurture, the child remains in or regresses to a sensation dominated state. Thus, emotional and cognitive developments are either halted or deteriorated. (p.10)

Tustin calls this state of mild autism 'a state of prethinking'. In the normal course of the early nurturing, relative satisfaction for both mother and baby predominates over negative feelings. Both are striving in response to biological drives – the baby for sustenance and the mother for their survival. Stressful situations occur from time to time but these are usually neither overwhelming nor prolonged. In these circumstances the infant can perceive regularities existing in the world around him and start the process of creating sufficient unity within himself. This fosters the gradual separation of the identities of mother and baby. Integration within the infant of a whole range of feelings and perceptions is only possible when a recognizable series can be discerned by the baby. The actual continuum that the baby has to cope with must not contain such extremes of intensity that they overwhelm the integrating process. As described by Tustin, a fundamental feeling of oneness representing the self emerges. Sometimes, the term 'containment' is used to describe the mediation of the mother which enables the baby to create an ordered system of ideas from the early state of unconnected sensory experiences.

For this basic state of wholeness to develop, the baby must not be dominated by overwhelming painful experience. Through a healthy give and take with the parents, the baby emerges as a distinct individual. This requires a reasonable level of sensitivity and consistency from the parents, that is, a reasonable level of maturity in dealing with the strong demands of a baby. During this period the family needs a supporting environment in terms of access to material resources as well as to secondary resources providing emotional support. They will then be able to rear the baby in a loving and reasonably consistent manner. This state of affairs produces the continuity which must exist before it can be perceived as such by the baby. This perceived continuity forms the basis for the construction of a system of whole objects, which produces sufficient equilibrium for intelligence to develop. The experiment described in the appendix draws attention to the possible effects of erratic maternal care on emergent concepts of constancy.

Piaget delineated the way in which intelligence develops systematically through the child's sensory experiences of continuity in relationships. Bowlby (1953) was concerned about the disastrous effects of discontinuity, mainly in the form of maternal deprivation. He observed that the outcome of such bad experience in the early years was unhappiness and often antisocial or psychopathic behaviour. His basic assertion is: 'What is believed to be essential for mental health is that the infant and young child should experience a warm, intimate and continuous relationship with his mother…in which both find happiness and enjoyment.' (p.75).

Between parent and infant, the mature parent is satisfied by being able to meet many, but certainly not all, of the demands of the offspring. Learning how to put up with frustration is an essential part of a child's development.

Give and take between parent and infant, together with continuity and the predominance of pleasure over dissatisfaction and pain, means that the conditions exist for the infant to create within itself a unified sense of identity. And such conditions do exist for most babies born into reasonably stable societies. If the nurturing environment is reasonably reliable and there is adequate attention paid to the child's individuality and vulnerability, a sense of wholeness develops. A stable vantage point, or centre of gravity, becomes lodged within the upright position.

Exploration of possible causes of the failure to create whole objects

When the continuity of a satisfying nurturing situation is broken up by overpowering sensations of pain and deprivation, the conditions necessary for integration or 'coming together' of fragmented sensations to form wholes does not exist. Instead of achieving the creative interaction of whole objects, what may remain is the sensation of part objects crashing together. Sometimes, the resulting internal state is referred to as a two-dimensional state of mind. In this state, before a solid three-dimensional world has been created, sensations related to surfaces are predominant. There can be no conception of spaces inside objects and space all around. There can be no understanding of time as this is logically dependent on the continued existence of objects, even when out of sight (Meltzer 1975).

For good development there must be a high level of predictability in the parents' attitude towards caring for the baby. Then, gradually, over time, the infant is able to perceive the adult as a whole being. If such nurturing conditions do not exist, experiences of neglect and deprivation (not to mention physical pain) alternating with satisfaction of need make the process of integrating sensory impressions very difficult. In these circumstances the carer does not function as a container to bring together all the disparate emotional experiences. Sometimes, what remains for the infant is a sense of emptiness – an aching void. At other times, extreme feelings of rage (power) erupt or there are feelings of weakness/vulnerability. Both extremes of experience remain isolated, uncontained and, therefore, without a self to take control.

The perception of whole objects involves interlinked emotional and intellectual development. The mother's wholeness means that she is capable of 'holding' the baby during the early months and years, during which time sense impressions are organized to form whole and distinct objects rather than fragmented sense impressions taking on heightened significance as indicated by Tustin. This applies to the child's conception himself and to that of those close to him. Failure of integration at this primary level, which results from overwhelmingly strong, uncontained distress, is very difficult to put right later. It leads to both intellectual and emotional impairment.

Adequate stability of nurturing may be disturbed in a variety of ways. Medical problems with either mother or baby might make their relationship difficult. Even where there are no complicating factors, the rearing of a child makes long-term demands on the parents. The nature of the outcome depends, to a large extent, on the degree to which the parents themselves are reasonably well integrated (internally and externally by productive social relationships) so that they have the capacity to contain and protect the totally dependent offspring. The parents need to be able to provide sufficiently stable conditions to facilitate the normal integrating process The context in which the child rearing takes place cannot be ignored. Social factors such as poverty and unemployment may have a devastating effect on parental health and behaviour.

Francis Tustin pointed out that for some children the non-integration results from a terror which paralyses. This is in accordance with the ideas of Piaget, i.e. that all interaction with the environment involves both structuring and valuation. For the baby, the most important 'object' is, usually, the mother. Sometimes, because the extremes of affect experienced by the infant are overwhelming, the perception of the underlying wholeness of form (of the mother) is obliterated. An understanding of the unitary nature of the self and of the mother will not be structured from such experiences, which do not form a continuum. Inherent discontinuity for the infant can have many different causes. Apart from separations, the mother may be physically or mentally ill. Early fragmented states tend to remain unresolved. This failure affects total development – all aspects of behaviour. The process of concept formation which unfolds in a systematic manner will be disrupted. This, of course, means that the ability to think sensibly is disabled and that there will be wide fluctuations in mood and behaviour. The twin effects of severe deprivation and/or abuse are intellectual and emotional.

Non-integration originating at the oral level: two illustrative cases

1. Lack of primary wholeness – severe feeding difficulties for a newly born infant produced extreme suffering and a sense of powerlessness

Jackie, as a baby, had never experienced the blissful feeling of containment described by Tustin. For Jackie, there had been an excess of pain resulting from medical problems associated with eczema and feeding difficulties compounded with the distress of maternal deprivation. At times of extreme discomfort and pain, the baby had lost touch with her mother. Just at those moments when she needed feeding and soothing ministrations she received the opposite – painful treatment of her sore skin. Jackie's mother felt rejecting towards the baby from birth.

Jackie was classified by psychologists as being intellectually retarded but it was the obvious emotional turmoil and distress which was the reason for her referral for weekly psychotherapy. The work of psychotherapy was towards linking the fragments of Jackie's experience and increasing her personal sense of value. During this belated struggle towards wholeness she brought into consciousness a part of herself which embodied painful and aggressive feelings. She even gave a name to this aspect of herself which carried a large amount of separated-off energy. She called him 'Squeaky Gream'.

She drew Squeaky Gream from time to time during the six years of her once-weekly treatment. During this time his form changed dramatically. At one point he was just a hole – an aching void. The sounds of these words connect with the noises that she made in her distress and to the hated cream which was applied to her painful skin.

Much later, Squeaky Gream became a whole figure with most features – in particular, he had a mouth full of teeth and was smiling and saying 'hello'. The efforts towards integration were important in order to make this valuable energy available to build up her sense of autonomy and worth. I think that the disastrous nurturing experience, which was akin to abuse, had damaged the budding sense of self. Those vitally important conditions to initiate the process of integration had been lacking. The sense of power and value had been denuded. Jackie's struggle towards wholeness is described more fully in the next chapter.

Experience at the other extreme is a form of engulfing of the infant which prevents separation of mother and child:

> The way in which the mother fulfils her role in the infant's struggle to form an ego is very important. Deprivation of need is not the only cause of schizoid withdrawal. Not only must the mother meet the infant's needs when he feels them, but she must not force herself on him in ways and at times that he does not want. That constitutes 'impingement' on the as yet weak, immature and sensitive ego of the infant. (Guntrip 1974, p.67)

A brief description of such a case follows, indicating the kind of consequences that are likely to result from over-impingement by the mother.

2. Domination of an infant resulting from a mother's wish to engulf an idealised child

In order for mother and infant to become whole objects for themselves and each other, they need to be able to separate. Diana's mother appeared to have been determined, from the beginning, to prevent this happening. She referred to her daughter as 'a carbon copy of myself', adding, 'she is my pride and joy'. From birth, Diana was adored by her mother, who tried to get her small beautiful baby to take in as much as possible of her ample supply of milk. She described how she used to wake the baby to feed her and that, frequently, excess milk would be vomited after a feed.

In her teens Diana was referred for bulimia. Food was the central area of conflict, but, in reality, there was a maternal determination to keep possession and control over the idealized child. Diana was doing quite well at school and she intended to continue her education. In this ambition she was supported by her mother, who envisaged that she would still remain at home whilst at college. She gave the impression that she had no intention of ever letting go of her daughter.

Diana's mother herself had been hospitalized earlier for depression and alcoholism which, she said, had resulted from her husband's physical and emotional abuse. She said that he used to dominate and humiliate her. They had been divorced for several years and lived separately. Nevertheless, he stayed with the family from time to time and he was the biological father of mother's third child, conceived after the divorce.

The father gave them quite regular financial support but this was hardly mentioned. Mother and daughter combined in their professed hatred for the father. Domination and abuse (including of food and alcohol) were a recurring theme in this complex family pattern. It was also characterized by extremes of ambivalence within each individual member. Judging by the way in which they behaved towards each other, respect for each other's individual integrity was minimal – as was self-esteem.

There seemed to be a need to dominate or manipulate others or, alternatively, to submit to the domination of others. Such patterns of relationships indicate a limited sense of personal worth and wholeness and a corresponding inability to respect and encourage the integrity of others. The relationships within the family operated at a part-object level.

The need for roots

Janet, in her early adolescence, was referred to the child guidance centre because she was being disruptive at school and at home. Amid the turmoil of adolescence were questions about her origins as she was obviously of mixed race in a family which was otherwise classified as 'white'. Questions arose

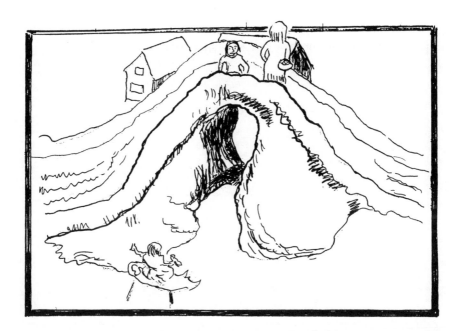

Figure 3.1: World in damp sand made by Janet about 13 years

because, for the parents, it had been easier to leave the matter unexplained. Such secrets within the family are hard for children to cope with.

Janet had even begun to doubt that her mother really was her mother. Janet became very creatively involved in her individual sessions and produced striking paintings and well-constructed Worlds in her exploration of how to think about and accommodate her own particular circumstances.

At one time her preoccupation with detritus such as apple cores, used sanitary towels and other 'rubbish', which she began to hoard, caused further disruption at home. This behaviour appeared to be, in part, a manifestation of her interest in her 'roots'. These matters were taken up within the family. It became evident that Janet had made progress after she had attended for about a year when she produced a simple, striking World in damp sand which showed a more comfortable feeling about herself and her family.

Janet used all the sand to form a large 'tunnel-bridge' on top of which she placed two figures – one represented herself, the other her mother. They were physically close together and, in a sense, united on top of the bridge but both were looking in opposite directions. Janet was looking at 'fairy-tale things', her mother at 'everyday things'. Janet was beginning to come to terms with herself and her position in the family. The fact that she was able to accept that her mother also had a point of view, though different from her own, showed a growing maturity. She was able to appreciate the integrity of others. Reports from school began to improve and she fairly soon discharged herself.

CHAPTER 4

Jackie
A fuller case study

This section is followed by an examination of play sequences revealing aspects of Jackie's struggle to create basic wholeness which needs a sense of uprightness at the core.

When I first met Jackie she was five years old. She had a place in a school for children who were emotionally disturbed as well as intellectually impaired. Her intelligence quotient was found to be in the low forties. In her special school she had been provided with a private 'den' where she could hide with her favourite comforter when she felt particularly vulnerable. It was her obvious emotional turmoil and distress which prompted her referral for psychotherapy at the local Child Guidance Centre.

Jackie's manner was oblique; her look was rather vague with an unfocused quality. Nevertheless, she gave out a sense of eagerness and need. She clearly appreciated the individual attention given to her during her weekly sessions. Her activities were, at first, repetitive and slow to evolve. She seemed to need a long period of time to build up a sense of trust. This was a measure of her early failure in basic nurturing.

The psychiatric social worker who worked with Jackie's mother learned just how disastrous had been Jackie's primary experience. As Jackie's therapist, I had indirect evidence of this and believe that the lack of organisation in her inner world was, at least partly, a direct result of this. It had affected both her intellectual and emotional development. The picture that gradually emerged was of an infant suffering pain and distress compounded by isolation as a result of her mother's inability to cope, her general aloofness and her turning away at times of extreme distress. On mother's part, there was almost certainly a degree of rejection, partly dealt with by denial.

Jackie's early history

Jackie was the middle child of three children. She had an older and a younger brother. Both Jackie and her mother managed to put on a bright, brave face. Mother smiled a lot but she was rather distant and conveyed little sense of real warmth in her attitude towards Jackie. Her manner was pleasant and business-like. Father seemed to take little share in the day-to-day care of the children.

Recorded events of the first year of Jackie's life, particularly the medical history, show that there had been little chance of a loving relaxed relationship developing between mother and baby. Jackie's mother's initial reaction to her (and to the birth itself) was in terms of strong feelings of undefined dissatisfaction. She knew that there was 'something wrong'. In her sessions with the social worker she recorded of a series of worrying problems.

At around two weeks Jackie went blue after a nappy change. She was crying a great deal and appeared to choke. Steps were taken to clear her passageways by shaking her upside-down. At three weeks there was unexplained diarrhoea which produced severe nappy rash and later there were breath-holding screams 'if angered', when Jackie would turn blue. At fourteen weeks the breast milk failed. This was put down to interrupted feed times due to 'other family commitments' but no arrangements were attempted to see that this did not happen. Shortly before the milk failed there had been the first unexplained vomit. This led to dehydration and hospitalization. This sequence – vomiting and hospitalization – occurred three times in all.

Twice, after the feeding routine had been stabilised in hospital, Jackie was returned home. Within a day or so the problem of vomiting returned. The hospital carried out a wide range of tests for infections and also for physiological causes, but no cause was found. On her third visit to hospital, when she was about six months, weaning from the bottle was achieved. Severe eczema was yet another symptom causing distress to mother and, particularly, to Jackie. Before each feed the miserable routine of attending to the painfully sore skin had to be carried out, accompanied by Jackie's screams.

Jackie's eczema was in evidence when she attended the clinic. Both Jackie and her mother had memories of the screaming which accompanied the regular bathing and anointing of her skin before each feed, when she was very hungry. So there was always an angry, painful prelude to what should have been a mutually satisfying experience. The screaming amplified the distress for both mother and baby. Aspects of this experience were worked on during Jackie's treatment – as described later.

The family doctor found that Jackie was 'retarded' at the age of three months. At four years of age, Jackie's mental age was assessed as being at about the level of a two-year-old. At the age of four and a half years she was referred for the first time to child guidance. At this time a child psychiatrist was reluctant to recommend psychotherapy because there was a lack of capacity for intellectual abstraction. About six months later she was taken on for individual psychotherapy because of the urgency of her need – for a trial period initially.

Jackie was described by her mother as being the kind of child who could not accept affection, cuddles or any form of physical restraint. So, when cuddling might have been called for, when she fell over as a toddler or when she was consumed with frustration and anger over some matter, mother would simply carry her to her cot with her favourite blanket and leave her to 'cry it out'.

Jackie's mother had another way of coping with difficult behaviour, including violent outbursts: she would turn away to compose herself before turning round to Jackie with a smile. She explained that she always tried to show a smiling face to Jackie. Sometimes, when she was feeling particularly upset, she would sing to try and gain composure and disguise the stress in her voice. She said that she believed that a loving atmosphere was good for development and that disapproval was harmful. Taken at face value, her attitude was loving and positive. Nevertheless, denial of feelings on both sides is obvious; in acute distress, the child was emotionally abandoned, at best she could see the back of her mother's head. The underlying despair of the mother, which probably had its roots in her own early history, had never been dealt with. But for Jackie, the feeling of being encircled by the loving presence of her mother was virtually lacking.

In Harry Guntrip's words, 'Reaction to deprivation involves, anger, hunger, sheer fear and withdrawal, and to these are added reaction to real external menace' (1968 p.12).

In school Jackie had temper tantrums. Sometimes she attacked smaller children or pulled boys' hair with great vehemence. Most of the time she could not bear the close proximity of other children, so a small 'den' was arranged for her to retreat to when she felt like doing so. Emotional contact with others, children as well as adults, was minimal. She appeared to be incapable of empathy.

When she first attended for treatment, her speech consisted mainly of the naming of objects and very short three-word phrases. She had a wide gait and a stomping walk. Her fine motor control was poor. Her eyes were filled with curiosity but they seldom rested anywhere for long. From time to time there were smiles and laughter. At these times she was capable of a sense of fun.

Most of the time she gave the impression of deprivation covered over with a brave attempt at control and self-sufficiency. Her skin continued to be very sensitive and dry. Often, there were red raw patches where she had scratched at her legs, hands or even her face.

The significance of spatial ideas: examples from Jackie's play

During early sessions the dominant theme was of falling down and being hurt. In Jackie's first two sessions she frequently banged the sides of her body using the palms of her hands. There was much shooting with a toy gun of the therapist and herself, accompanied by laughter. Both had to fall down. Her play was repetitive and ritualistic with gradual modifications. Much of it was concerned with vehicles crashing into each other, with these objects falling and being hurt. For example, the bus would be in a crash. It would roll over and lie down, hurt – 'Poor Bus'.

She sometimes carried the red fire engine, tenderly, after it had 'fallen down', to the dolls house, where it was placed on its side on the 'soft' carpet to 'snuggle down' and 'go to sleep'. I think that the redness of the fire engine reminded her or her own painful feelings, and was the same colour as her damaged skin. It represented the hurt and damaged self in need of soothing containment. Resting inside the safety of the doll's house, I thought it represented her wish to be encircled and comforted. With hindsight, I now think she might have been showing me her need to get away from some hurtful, real situation.

During the first two years of treatment Jackie's play continued to be fragmentary. It was the play of a child who, for the most part, felt herself to be the victim of outside forces which she could in no way control or comprehend. There was a recurrence of crashing and of being down and hurt. The way in which Jackie and her mother came together from the beginning was, on the emotional level, like two objects crashing, hurting each other. I would now give serious consideration to the possibility that Jackie, at a later stage, had been abused other than verbally by a sibling. The fact that handicapped children are more likely to be abused than normal children has been brought into the open by such workers in the field of child psychotherapy as Valerie Sinason.

It might have been said about Jackie that she had a low sense of self-esteem. But, as her sense of self, as a distinct entity, was hardly formed, the statement is not apt. She was still in the primary stage, struggling towards establishing herself as a whole person. The awareness of herself and others as solid three-dimensional objects was dimly emerging. It was as if fragments of experience overlapped two-dimensionally and needed organising into three-dimensional wholes. This state of existing virtually precludes feelings of empathy. Confidence in the reality of herself and others was so shaky that an understanding of causality and of time had not been established. Such ideas flow from the appreciation of the solidness of objects.

Jackie's speech was correspondingly retarded. The words 'tomorrow' and 'yesterday' were not understood and, of course, she never used them. She was unable to use pronouns and she had not reached the stage of being able to distinguish between animate and inanimate objects. She once drew a house in the form of a large rectangular face with two eyes (with eyebrows) in the top corners, a straight line for the nose and a curving mouth.

Lack of connections within Jackie's inner world

One way in which the fragmented nature of Jackie's inner word revealed itself was in her fear of vacuum cleaners and other noisy machines. She reacted as if they were monsters out to get her in one way or another. She invested them with that range of powerful negative energies identical with those which had overwhelmed her when she had had to cope with pain and hunger whilst in a state of emotional isolation. This state of being, without a sense of containment, of not knowing what was inside or what was outside, had prevailed since she was born. Around the void created by pain and grossly inadequate mothering, 'good' and 'bad' energies remained separated off from each other. There was no internal 'coming together' to unite disparate sensations and create a whole.

Jackie was very afraid of the vacuum cleaners, partly because of the noise and also because there were ideas about being sucked in along with all the dirt. Together with the sense of badness and rejection was the feeling of powerlessness. I did wonder at the time what the effect would have been if her mother had been able to show Jackie how to switch the machine on and off. It might have moved the emphasis away from being the passive victim towards being able to exert power. Mother's attitude seemed always to be one of brave resignation and would not have included any such approach to Jackie.

Jackie also had a similar fear of the tractor which pulled a grass cutter. She took a keen interest in the daisies and grass cut down by the machine. She picked up bits of cut grass, held them delicately in the air and watched the wind blow them away. This interest echoed her feelings about having her hair cut. In a play sequence, described more fully in a later section, the hair being cut was associated with the pain and deprivation which was the girl's lot, not the boy's. Much later in treatment she had further ideas about things being cut. She said that tractors had 'blades' (she had just learned this new word) and told me that her mother also had blades which she used to cut vegetables. There was quite an intensity behind her interest in blades and their function.

The noise made by machines was, for Jackie, their most frightening feature. I think that the noise was experienced as being of a similar quality to the sound of her own screaming, which she would have heard when she had been in a highly distressed state as a hungry infant. At that time she would have had no comprehension of the source of the noise. The screaming would have been just another sensation impinging on her inner state of fear and pain. Although the sense of self as an entity had not been formed, her crying must have been experienced, in some way, as harsh and persecutory.

For a long time the main feeling she expressed during her sessions was of an awareness of being 'down', as has been described earlier. Objects having fallen down or crashed into were damaged and hurt as a result. The main idea conveyed was of being a passive victim.

Play sequences which demonstrate Jackie's efforts towards basic integration

The use of movement in the visual creation of whole objects, that is, the manipulation of an object in order to observe the transformations

In a chapter about the child's development of an understanding of the spatial field, Piaget (1954) reports his observation of the way in which a child, aged around ten months, actively manipulates objects horizontally, and in depth, in order to visually study their transformations.

To engage in this activity, Jackie used to perch herself on the edge of my chair. This meant that we both had a similar view of the visual transformations to be brought about by Jackie. First, she used a large baby doll. She held it at eye level, starting with a back view, and moved it slowly forwards and then gradually turned it round, scrutinising it all the time. At first, she carried out these movements in silence. I talked about the doll going away and coming back. Jackie later said 'goodbye' and 'hello' as the doll came back. Re-establishing eye contact between Jackie and the baby doll was of great importance during this manoeuvre. The fact that Jackie's mother had a habit of turning away at moments of great stress must surely be relevant to this need which Jackie had to work on in this kind of visual sequencing. This activity was engaged in over a number of weeks. It was carried out in silence most of the time, slowly and in a calm and thoughtful manner. It was as if, by her movements, she was visually confirming the constancy of objects. Such constancy is one of the first forms of the concept of conservation. By means of this active and creative play, Jackie was relating together visual impressions in a meaningful way to form wholes.

Later during this period when she scrutinised figures in different positions she used small dolls in a crouching position. Here the focus of interest was at the pelvic level. Sexual differentiation was of intense interest to Jackie. Gradually her passionate wish to be a boy came into focus. From her point of view, the boy not only had a penis but he was fed with good milk, whilst she had 'smelly' ointment and painful experience.

One of Jackie's strengths was her visual acuity in relation to detail. Though her language development and, of course, her comprehension skills were poor, she learned to read, write and spell quite well during the time she was in treatment. This visual acuity was, perhaps, symptomatic of a more serious disability – her restricted capacity to comprehend the wider view. This may link to the difficulty in creating whole objects and mean that only part objects are available with which to relate. The dawning of self-awareness occurs when sufficient integration has developed over time, between what was originally a succession of sensory events. The restriction of perception to unconnected detail is illustrated in the next example of Jackie's play. The subsequent gradual widening of perception allowed integration of different facets of experience.

Another example of movement – the movement of dry sand through a funnel

Jackie observed the movement of the sand with great concentration. When Jackie first played with dry sand, pouring it through a large funnel, she concentrated on the build-up of sand inside the funnel, noticing how it slipped down in the centre. It was some time before she was able to widen her perception to notice, and take an interest in, the outflow of sand. Gradually, over time, her perception expanded and she was able to link both ends of the process and to 'see' that as the sand goes in at the top, it flows out at the bottom. The concept of space and spaces emerges. This leads towards understanding of 'inside' and 'outside' – a novel connection for Jackie. Perceiving the flow through the funnel is, for example, analogous to the movement between mouth and anus. It is a comprehension which marks the threshold between two-dimensional and three-dimensional structuring and, consequently, in the formation of whole objects. Following on is the dawning awareness of 'front' and 'back', 'top' and 'bottom'. The idea of objects having contents becomes a possibility; it becomes possible to think about feelings, which are also 'inside'.

It is no coincidence that around this time she sometimes filled the dumper truck with sand and dumped loads of sand near the dolls house. This led on to talk about babies being 'smelly', according to Jackie. In this talk she was trying to reject the vulnerable 'bad' aspects of herself. A fuller understanding of this came later. This ability to begin to take a larger view of her position was noticeable at the end of her third year of treatment. She began to bring her feelings into focus and to show how she experienced her relationships within the family. Very gradually, ideas emerged, such as the opposing qualities of good and bad and the complex ways in which they exist together.

When Jackie was almost nine years old her play began to involve relatively whole objects. She took two large baby dolls, one of which was a sexed 'boy' doll, and seated them in the dry sand tray. She dramatised the way in which a mother cared for, and fed, her two babies. In this way she made explicit her own awareness of privation. The sexed boy doll was seated at one end of the dry sand tray and the girl baby doll at the other. She poured dry sand through a funnel to fill two bottles. As on earlier occasions, one bottle was referred to as 'milk' and the other bottle and its contents were referred to as 'cream' – by which she meant ointment for eczema. She frequently sniffed the 'cream' and pronounced it to be 'horrible'. She demonstrated how to pour it out into the palm of her hand and rubbed it (sand) into the back of her hand, which was often dry and sore. Then she became 'mother'. The boy was attended to first. He was cuddled, given milk and his hair was stroked, as was his penis. Mother supplied him with all good things. On the other hand, the baby girl was told that she would have her food 'in a minute'. The baby girl was supplied with other things first. 'Smelly' cream was rubbed into her leg, 'to make it better'. Then the baby girl's hair was cut. She was comforted a little but she was not given milk. Jackie's statement was pretty clear: the boy has access to the good things whilst the girl suffers pain and privation.

Figure 4.1: Drawing by Jackie

'Squeaky Greem is crying.' His eyes are closed. Tears are falling to the bottom of the page. Jackie's foot, touching the top of Squeaky Greem's head, is pushing him down.

The emergence of a vital, split-off segment of Jackie's personality

The emergence of 'Squeaky Gream' occurred at the beginning of the third year of treatment. He embodied all the painful, desolate and angry feelings which had never been incorporated, all the 'bad' angry feelings connected with the misery of the pre-feeding routine when, in her state of hunger, her painful eczema was treated. Jackie drew him with a round head and a square body. He had neither legs nor arms. His eyes were closed but tears were falling down his face and all over the rest of the paper. His mouth was open. Jackie's foot was shown in the drawing (upper right, touching the head). It was a round foot attached to part of her leg. The rest of her body was missing. She said that the foot was 'pushing him down', that is, Squeaky Gream. This shows how, at this point, she externalised parts of herself which were persecutory and in conflict, relating to past experience. This indicates the state of her inner world inhabited by 'part objects'. They represented active and passive aspects of herself.

These are Jackie's words of explanation:

> Tip up lorry crashed the milk float
> Milk float fighting.
> Squeaky Gream punch on Jackie's tummy.
> Jackie is cry in the garden.
> Jackie step on the Squeaky Gream.

The immaturity of the language is part of her restricted comprehension. She still referred to herself in the third person, being unable to use the words 'you' and 'I'. During this session she talked about the sex of various toys. 'Pick-up truck is a boy', drawing attention to the crane. She also said that the house was 'a very good boy' and the garage was 'a very, very good girl'. She had an excellent memory for names. She could remember the names of all the children in her school and usually mentioned their sex as well.

A few months later Jackie drew Squeaky Gream again. This time he was just an empty round shape, a void. He was totally bereft. She said that he had no ears, no mouth, nothing! (also no eyes). He represented a state of privation and desolation, the void both inside and outside, shared by both mother and infant. There may be some similarity with 'the black hole' (Tustin 1972 p.34).

Though Squeaky Gream was still a split-off entity, Jackie was beginning to be able to own her unhappy experiences and could link him to them. Later, she talked about him being run over by a lorry after he had been thrown out in the road. So the images of being pushed down, flattened down, were still the dominant ones. There were few images, as yet, of the upright object symbolic of the emergent self.

Development in Jackie's play was very gradual. She had briefly identified herself with the mother of the boy and girl babies so she was beginning to be able to integrate a different point of view, one where she had the power to act upon others. There was one activity, which she discovered during her weekly session, which both of us enjoyed. Jackie became the teacher in charge of music and movement. She banged the drum in fast or slow rhythm. She watched with pleasure how I responded by trotting or walking in time with her beat.

Movement towards a more 'upstanding' position representing a degree of power centred in an emerging self

One item of play which indicated a rise in Jackie's spirits was when she had placed conkers in the large sieve. She enjoyed making them bounce up and down by quickly jerking the sieve up and down. A week or so later she chose to use the woodwork tools to do 'a bit of sawing', also hammering and drilling.

She said that she was being 'like a man'. During the same session she also took on the role of shopkeeper, also a man. I was told to be the woman who went to get things from the shop. Jackie had absolutely no idea how money transactions worked but she was showing greater fluidity of thought and imagination. She enjoyed the role of shopkeeper because she was expanding her own feeling of worth by identifying with the shopkeeper who was in control of the source of valuable supplies. This was in marked contrast with her earlier preoccupation with privation. She was beginning, at times, to identify with the powerful individual, one who had access to all the good things, who might even be the aggressor.

Around this time she was becoming more explicit about her wish to be a boy. This wish was absolutely understandable. As a girl, and for other reasons, she had suffered denigration of various forms within the family. One day she arrived announcing that she was not Jackie any longer. She gave herself the name of a boy that she knew. Incidentally, he was a boy against whom she had always had strong feelings. Whilst always letting her know that I had some understanding of her urgent wish to be a boy, I told her that the person that I wanted to see was Jackie herself. Also, for what it was worth, that neither I nor her mother had any control over who was to be a boy or a girl. Also, I said that I had no wish to see the boy she had named. After a few weeks the idea of taking another name was dropped. I tried to encourage other people to stop asking her 'Who are you today Jackie?' This is a question which seems to promote the splitting process rather than help the work of integration.

At the core of wholeness is a sense of uprightness, which provides a vantage point for observation, contemplation and action

Jackie was engaged in a struggle to create a 'whole' self. As yet, her internal world was not so much two-dimensional as pre-three-dimensional.

When the self becomes a sufficiently stabilized entity, the perpendicular is a central feature of a three-dimensional understanding which includes such notions as the sequencing of sensory data over time creating constancy of shape, and so forth. A centre of control (the self) provides focus and a degree of stability from which an organising function can be maintained.

Within this central area, accessible to consciousness, an attempt is made to settle for what is important or valued. The capacity to behave autonomously develops. The individual attempts to make sense of (and to exert influence on) his world. Provided a degree of consistency in external relationships creates wholeness during the primary developmental stage, this attempt is successful. But, if the embryonic organising self is cleft by some overwhelming experience, all kinds of extreme experiences remain unconnected. Fragments, deriving from these uncontained experiences, disrupt thinking, feeling and, of course, behaviour. An inability to relate sensations together to form wholes means that functioning is equally unco-ordinated, reflecting the lack of global understanding.

CHAPTER 5

Difficulties over autonomy and a sense of direction

Finding direction – an attribute of wholeness

A good adaptation to reality, a sense of autonomy and a reasonably consistent direction in life develops very gradually, based on good nurturing experience, which promotes integration and a strong sense of self. To bring this about, helping the child to learn how to comply with normal social constraints needs to have been carried out with great care in order to respect growing capacities.

The child is then able to take over ever-increasing responsibility for his own actions and well-being. This can only happen in a social setting which itself functions as an integrated whole, where tensions and even conflicts, when they occur, are worked though to a resolution. In other words, the society would function with a degree of consensus. This raises other questions, one of which is: 'How many families and/or societies do function in something like an integrated way, with respect for individuals?'

Healthy development in a child depends upon the regular input of resources, that is, a great deal of effort from carers. A positive outcome is achieved when the child perceives the self and others as a whole entities. This understanding forms the basis for an understanding of causality and of time as a directional concept.

> The primary drive in every human being is to become a 'person', to achieve a solid ego formation, to develop a personality in order to live. This can only be done in the medium of personal object relationships. (Guntrip 1968, p.174)

A developing sense of wholeness, uniqueness and autonomy within the child promotes a degree of confidence, 'knowing where they are going'. There are many difficulties in the way of this being achieved, given all the complexities of life and the rapidity of social change. All these discontinuities tend to destroy the element of predictability and the feeling of underlying support on which creative social life depends. In such circumstances, it becomes difficult for the individual to establish a sense of self. Guidano says:

'Perception of an irreversible directedness of time is essential in the structuring of human experience. This perception forms the foundation of our sense of causality and its characteristic directionality always has the cause preceding the consequence never vice versa'. (1987, p.12)

He goes on to say that a temporal sense of direction – from past to present and from present to future – is a requisite for developing goal-seeking behaviour. Such structured understanding is essential in dealing effectively with reality. This understanding is built on the solid foundation of a 'good-enough' system of whole objects experienced in childhood.

Three possible causes of passive regression

Guntrip (1968) examines aspects of what he calls the struggle to preserve the ego. He identifies three possible causes for a healthy, outgoing approach to life being replaced by passive regression, summarised here:

1. *Tantalising refusal* by those responsible for the infant to satisfy his libidinal needs.

2. *Impingement* of a hostile or aggressive object or situation arouses direct fear of an overpowering outer world and evokes withdrawal as a flight into the inner world.

3. *Rejection and neglect*, non-recognition or desertion, by the outer world…leaves the infant facing, as it were, a vacuum in which it is impossible to live. (p.75)

These three causes, which undermine the development of autonomy, are really failures in the environment to provide the necessary supplies. Again we see how the internal and the external interlock.

The individual who suffers pain through inherently hostile actions feels 'put down', denuded of power. These three external conditions, itemised by Guntrip, might now be classified as forms of abuse: deprivation, physical abuse or emotional abuse. All result from the exercise of power external to the sufferer. Directly or indirectly, energy outside works against the individual in his struggle for survival.

Access to various forms of essential supplies, if denied to the totally dependent infant, produces forms of turning inward, rather than outward with a degree of optimism. If such deprivations occur at a very early stage in development, the initial containment on which the whole process depends may be destroyed. If abuse occurs at a later stage, the sense of wholeness is damaged, making productive action difficult.

Guntrip makes the observation that hydraulic and spatial metaphors are a handy way of envisaging the invisible process of change from extraversion to introversion. He adds that the process becomes visible enough when it is an accomplished fact, in the sense that 'the outflowing and unimpeded activity on which the whole of the healthy ego development depends, is precisely what has been overlaid by fear, choked back and dammed in, in the schizoid personality' (p.87).

Within expressive play material we find such spatial ideas made tangible so that they can be looked at and recorded during therapy and discussed and thought about as the exploration of therapy continues. Spatial ideas are such a fundamental form of thinking, it seems, that the term 'metaphor' gives the impression that they are more superficial than they actually are. Spatial ideas are an approximation to the form imposed on inner life, forged by powerful experiences in the real world, part of a deep inner structure.

Examples from clinical material, illustrating difficulties in achieving a strong enough sense of self to settle to a course of action

'The determined drive backwards'

Peter developed a perverse sense of direction, caused by traumatic early relationships, which made subsequent creative interaction with others all but impossible. The normal growth pattern, which should ensure a build-up of skill in coping with real situations, had been perverted by 'hostile impingement.'

Peter, described below, consistently exhibited 'The determined drive backwards', characteristic of the regressed ego (Guntrip 1979).

From information gathered from his mother, I think that Peter probably had quite a good initial start in life but, at an early stage, probably as a toddler, he had suffered the shock of harsh treatment from his father. This, coupled with over-protective indulgence from his mother and his father's subsequent total desertion, had disrupted Peter's sense of integrity and direction, producing what may be termed 'the regressed ego'. He had been referred for assessment for psychotherapy by his school.

Peter was the first-born child of a failed marriage. His mother was strongly involved with him. At the initial interview she said that she wanted treatment for him 'to make him happier'. He responded quickly by saying that he was happy already, and strongly denied having any problems. He said that the only thing that troubled him was that other boys were always fighting and he would like everything to be 'nice and quiet'. He attended regularly once a week with his mother.

Peter's father had been in the armed forces, on active service. According to Peter's mother, he had been a man of extreme mood swings. She reported that he had once reacted violently towards Peter when, as a small boy, he had shown resentment towards his very young brother. According to her description of father's reaction, it had been harsh in the extreme. The divorce and subsequent relationship was acrimonious. He refused to maintain contact with the children.

Peter was generally considered to be an intelligent boy, both by his teachers and his mother, but it was difficult to get him to work and his actual attainment was poor. He seemed to understand the mechanics of reading but he could not apply this and was unable to read fluently. It was a rather similar picture in relation to arithmetical calculations, which, superficially, he appeared to understand. He worked very slowly, and inaccurately, because he managed to reverse the mechanical process frequently.

This idea of going into reverse came up frequently, in connection with various topics. He had thoughts about getting smaller or thinner and being able to go through a letter box. His imagination had been captured by the film *Back to the Future.* He was mentioned on pp.39–40 because of his interest in ruins. Here again his interest was not in building a castle but, instead, he liked to mime a castle falling down or paint a ruined castle which he said had been knocked down by a giant. Things always seemed to be reducing or moving in a backward or downward direction.

Peter's mother complained that if he was told *not* to do something, Peter tended to do it. One day she arrived irate for the session because Peter had fed the dog, which was being prepared for a visit to the vet. Strict instructions had been given out not to feed it.

This perverse approach seemed to pervade most aspects of his behaviour – it had become a well-organised character trait. After attending with his mother for several weeks, he drew the picture reproduced in Chapter 2. It showed himself standing triumphantly on a cliff top whilst two other figures were falling down to the bottom of the cliff face. The falling figures represented significant 'other' people in his life, perhaps his mother and his therapist.

Peter's mother also bemoaned the fact he was unable to express his sadness about what had happened to himself and his family in relation to the desertion by his father. Perhaps she was asking him to express these feelings for her. In some way she seemed to look on him as still being part of herself. She had a high opinion of his intelligence but was exasperated by his behaviour. He was almost nine years old and he still had to be taken to school. He was unable to follow instruction about how to cross roads safely. As a busy mother, who also worked, she tended to lose her temper with him. At school also his behaviour caused a lot of irritation. It was as if he was busy undoing what the teachers were trying to do, trying to reduce them to a state of impotence, as had happened to himself in relation to his father and, perhaps, also his mother.

One day he drew a strange diagram of a big bird at the bottom of a square hole, as if being looked down on. He said that its beak was wide open. Just the outline of its open beak could be seen, as from above, at the bottom of the hole. He said that the bird was waiting for some food to be dropped into its beak. In a mildly puzzled way I said that I thought that big birds usually get their own food. He replied: 'This one has had his wings clipped.' Peter seemed to have quite a high level of insight into his own situation. The picture of the bird gives a depressingly definite view of how passive Peter felt about his access to the source of supplies. It reveals also just how strong was the feeling of damage done to himself and the incapacity and impotence that Peter was working against.

The enmeshed relationship with his mother made it difficult to help him to modify his entrenched negative approach to himself and others. He modelled in plasticine the figure of a boy balanced on a skateboard, floating on the sea, close to a large whale with an open mouth. There was a recurring theme about moving backwards, perhaps back inside his mother?

Peter's relationship with his mother was, in large measure, the problem that needed tackling, but seeing them together did not appear to produce useful insight in either Peter or his mother. Even if he had been seen separately, his mother would still have remained a force to be reckoned with. With hindsight, I now think that I should have taken his initial strong denial of having any problem much more seriously. He resolutely maintained this attitude of denial. He continued his established way of being active and powerful by neutralising the efforts of other people, particularly if they were attempting to teach or influence him.

> The regressed ego denotes, not a freely available generalised 'fear and flight' reaction but the deepest structurally specific part of the complex personality, existing in a settled attitude of fear, weakness, withdrawal, and absolute dependence not in the active post-natal infantile sense but in a passive ante-natal sense. It represents the most profoundly traumatised part of the personality and is the hidden cause of all regressive phenomena...
> (Guntrip 1968, p.77)

Peter's mother, being the one who claimed to be motivated in an attempt to 'make him happy', always attended with him. After a time I had the impression that she derived a rather perverse pleasure out of the fact that I was making no progress in my attempt to help Peter become an agent in his own right. I was a rival, someone who was trying to do something which she had been unable to do. During one session Peter and his mother performed a war chant together, which excluded me, emphasising their solidarity. Referring back to the drawing Peter made of himself standing on the cliff top, watching the descent of therapist and mother, it was as if his mother had now joined him on the cliff top whilst I continued to fall alone.

The case was closed some time later with little sign that Peter was making progress towards extricating himself and moving positively towards experience. 'The rebirth and regrowth of the lost living heart of the personality is the ultimate problem psychotherapy now seeks to solve.' (Guntrip 1968, p.12).

Body-image distortion resulting from inappropriate parental relationships

'We are three dimensional organisms characterised by front-back, right-left, and top-bottom, and we structure space in terms of height, width, and depth' (Guidano 1987, p.7).

The Goodenough man drawing test was used for many years as a simple but fairly reliable way of assessing a child's level of functioning. Representations of the body do seem to be a good indicator of feelings about the self, which is, in turn, responsive to the degree of respect experienced. Impingement is likely to show up in terms of distortions in the body image.

Christine aged nine years, mentioned on p.30, (she pictured a girl who fell into a muddy pool) was a child who declared that she had secrets that she would never reveal to anyone. Her relationship to both parents was very close, particularly her father. She had great difficulty in getting to school. When coerced into doing so, she would scream outside the headmistress' office until she was taken home. During treatment she revealed that she had extreme fear connected with her dead grandfather who used to live with the family. He had died in the home. Christine now thought of him as being in heaven and thereby able to look down on her and observe what she was doing. She was afraid that he might report her misdeeds to God himself. Then she would be made ill. She produced an extremely distorted drawing of the human body (Figure 5.1). I think that the distortion resulted from some kind of sexual abuse, the exact nature of which remained her secret. The image of the grandfather, up in heaven, was again of an outside force willing to do her harm.

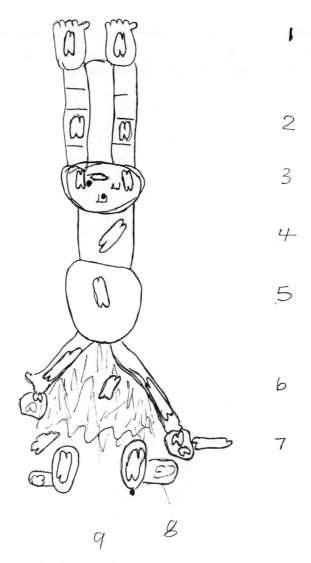

Figure 5.1: Drawing by Christine aged 9 years

1. Feet and bones
2. Legs
3. Mouth, nose, eyes and bones
4. Back and bone
5. Tummy and bone
6. Arms and bone
7. Shoulders and bone
8. Shoes, bones and buckles
9. Arms, hair and bone

John, aged eight, was referred for treatment because he had an inexplicable fear that clowns *might* unexpectedly make an appearance. This fear was ever-present, extreme and disruptive It struck him from time to time in school or when the family were on holiday. John was the younger child with an older

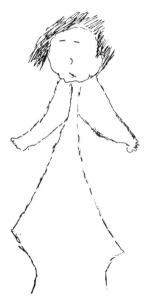

Figure 5.2: A drawing of a man by John aged 8 years

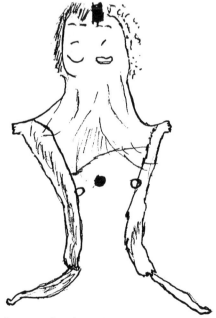

Figure 5.3: A drawing of a woman by John aged 8 years

sister who was getting on quite well. His mother seemed to be unusually insensitive to his feelings. He once came to the clinic with sore, untreated blisters on his feet.

Throughout his childhood, until fairly recently, he had slept in the parental bedroom. When his father went on business trips abroad, John would sleep with his mother. Over-involvement, through closeness to the sexual behaviour of his parents, and an inappropriately close relationship with his mother appeared to be the main cause of John's confusion and anxiety. The severity of his symptoms suggested that the full nature of his mother's behaviour towards him was not known. The distorted drawing of the female body was made early in treatment.

Damage done to the sense of self by abuse: A case study of Sidney

Sidney was referred for therapy at the age of eight. His parents were separated. He lived with his mother but his father took him out regularly and gave him money (only after Sidney was taken into residential care was the disclosure made that his father had been abusing him from an early age.) Sidney's symptoms were wetting and soiling from the age of three. Before this age he had been clean and dry. His father was an alcoholic who had also been abusive towards his very young wife, the mother of Sidney. An incident of sexual abuse by a much older boy when Sidney was six was reported by his mother. There was no suggestion from her that there was anything unusual about Sidney's relationship with his father. She herself rewarded Sidney for good behaviour by allowing him to sleep in her bed. In school, as well as lack of progress with formal skills, there were behavioural problems. One particular problem, reported from school, was that he refused to write or use a pencil.

At times Sidney could be disarmingly compliant and pleasant. But at other times, during his treatment sessions, also at school and at home, he revealed an almost uncontrollable wish to inflict hurt upon others. He threatened other children with scissors in the classroom. It is probable that the extremes of Sidney's behaviour mirrored that of his father towards him. To Sidney, his father was both a caring and an attacking adult. Though he exhibited a verbal precocity by his use of adult phrases, his thought processes and concepts were fractured. His patterns of thought were confused and illogical. Statements he made were often contradictory. For example, a girl much older than himself, who assisted his mother with minding the children, at times prevented him from playing with his own toys and hurt him physically. Sidney called this girl 'my friend'. Sidney's mother appeared not to notice the rather sadistic slant of the girl's attention, just as she was apparently unaware of the abuse inflicted on Sidney by his father from an early age.

The fractured nature of Sidney's external and internal world was graphically illustrated by the way he attacked his drawings with scissors. During his first year of treatment he was inhibited to such an extent that he was unable to use a pencil for writing or drawing. After about a year he tentatively began to use a pencil to draw small figures in simple pictures. He then started to use scissors to cut up what he had just created. This destruction would be followed by a frantic attempt to stick the picture back together again, using Sellotape. This always proved to be difficult (as with Humpty Dumpty).

Figure 5.4: A figure drawn by Sidney aged about 8 years

This is one of a series illustrating how, having drawn a figure, he would chop it up and try to reassemble it. This figure was stuck onto a fresh sheet of paper.

The first time Sidney followed this procedure he drew a small, rather squashed figure. This was first cut out, separating the figure from its background. Then the scissors were used to cut straight across the middle of the figure (later the two halves were cut into smaller fragments). Then he would try to re-assemble the separated parts by sticking them together onto another piece of paper.

(A self-portrait by Francis Bacon shows a fractured sense of self. Bacon's attitude to life was, in many ways, negative and lacked a sense of wholeness. He was preoccupied with thoughts about death and images of bestiality, of slaughterhouses and of raw and decaying flesh. He did not see life and death as part of a cycle, tied into other systems in the natural world.)

At other times Sidney would use the same method to try and re-establish a small upright figure between a strip of grass and the sky by sticking all three pieces back in place onto a fresh sheet of paper (having cut them away from their first setting). Watching these efforts to get the little figure back between earth and sky created in me an impression of being tossed around, unable to regain balance. It was something akin to the sensation of vertigo mentioned in Chapter 2.

(Those who have studied the activity of seeing, remark on the fact that, when we look around scanning a scene, taking in a succession of overlapping images, we still experience the world around us as being still and motionless. The stability of our world remains secure, in spite of the series of blurred visual images coming from our retina. The stability of our inner world has been created over a lifetime.)

Sidney was a boy whose inner self had been literally chopped up by bad experience, which overwhelmed him. At the opening of this chapter I quoted Guntrip's statement about there being a primary drive in every human being to become a 'person'. He goes on to say that this is achieved in the medium of personal object relationships. Given reasonably good conditions, the parent is able to contain and support the child. It is manifestly true that no parent who was reasonably well integrated could have behaved towards a child as Sidney's father did towards him. I never met Sidney's father, nor did the social worker involved. But, judging by his behaviour, I would think that he himself was a severely damaged individual. The pattern of relationships within the family seemed to be at the level of part objects crashing together. In this way, fragmented external reality and internal reality interlock. Sidney was removed from home because he was a threat to his young sister and his behaviour at school had not improved.

Graham was a boy who had a long-lasting problem over soiling

At around age ten he produced a Lego car which embodied his directional confusions, bodily and otherwise. The car had four wheels on top and four on the bottom. It could move upside down and in reverse. He did not respond well to individual therapy and the family background was something of a mystery.

Environmental conditions perpetuating fragmentation

Family organisation

In making an analysis of a child, some psychotherapists take pride in not being seduced by knowledge of actual events in the subject's life. But others think that it is essential to know as much as possible about the child's history and background. The following case summary illustrates the usefulness of this latter approach.

A girl named Clare, who was around eight years old, was referred for treatment at the child guidance centre because of odd behaviour and lack of progress at her special school. She was generally out of touch with what was going on around her. She displayed jerky arm movements, but, in spite of her twitches, she was remarkably good at drawing, particularly human figures.

From time to time, while playing with the doll's house, Clare mentioned thieves in the house, who even had tea with the family in the garden. I wondered about their presence. Clare eventually made a series of three rapid sketches in explanation of the existence of the robbers. The first drawing showed two women together, the second showed one of them holding a knife over the other and the third drawing was of the same woman lifting a baby up high. My knowledge of the events in the background of the family made it clear to me that these expressions were not examples of fantasy. It proved to be important for me to know that Clare's grandmother (with whom the family still lived) had, in the past, been a 'back-street abortionist' who had spent time in prison. Such illegal practitioners were fairly common in deprived inner-city areas where lack of contraceptive advice was one aspect of the general impoverishment. Clare's mother had grown up in a furtive atmosphere which 'smelt of carbolic soap'. In all our lives, events from the past, which have fashioned our inner worlds, project their effects into the future.

Clare's mother was anxious to protect her daughter from the unsavoury family history. Clare's reaction to this attempt at protection was a rather 'mad' detachment. During treatment Clare did not bring up ideas about her family background verbally. She demonstrated her situation of not being allowed to 'see' or 'know' by dramatisation using a teenage doll. A girl was undressing 'out of sight' behind an improvised screen. As Clare took clothes off the doll, she could not 'see' what her hands were doing. This literally displayed the state of disassociation which prevented Clare from being able to learn. She and her mother had had to adapt to an intense conflict within their lives, centred on the criminal behaviour of the grandmother. It was also reported that Clare's brother had suffered some form of sexual abuse.

By the time Clare attended for treatment, abortions were being carried out by the National Health Service and the subject of abortion was frequently in the news. This form of abortion was one of the topics which came up for brief mention during sessions. Clare responded well to psychotherapy and, after about a year of weekly sessions, she had made sufficient progress to move back to a normal school.

Deprived social conditions

Illegal abortions were carried out in the impoverished sections of society where access to information about contraception was hard to come by and even married women frequently feared having more children when they already had insufficient money to live on. Medical advice of all kinds, and treatment, would have been expensively out of reach. So the ramifications of Clare's problem extended beyond the family to the wider social setting.

Parents living in an unstable environment shot through with conflict find it difficult to provide continuity of nurturing for the immature infant. Such families exist in a state of internal and external fragmentation, not passed on via the genes but perpetuated over generations through a history of social deprivation. We will return to this topic in the next chapter.

Where the process of maturation is stunted as a result of bad nurturing or where abuse causes fragmentation, actions are likely to be haphazard or unpredictable, with scant regard for anyone's long-term interests. The same individual tends to be both the victim and the perpetrator of destructive social forces, both part of a vicious cycle. This would tend to suggest that individuals living in a state of lack of a cohesive inner self would not be capable of drawing ideas into consciousness and of becoming aware of conflict. Only then would they be able to arrive at a resolution which allowed a settled course of action. Behaviour would tend to be volatile. Action would result from whatever happened to be the current strongest impulse. They would be revealing their lack of inner connections, dealing with part objects.

People who develop and live under such conditions of privation and confusion have little or no influence over their personal destiny. Those low down in the social hierarchy which marginalises them have to cope with privations and fluctuating economic conditions as best they can, without the cushioning effect of having reserves to call upon.

Writers such as Irvine Welsh describe the day-to-day lives of people seriously addicted to heroin living in a deprived area of Edinburgh. Through the use of drugs, they exist within the movement back and forth between violently contrasting moods – the extremes of 'high' and 'low'. Preoccupation with the need to procure the drug alternates with experiencing its effects. This swing back and forth ensures that they are contained within this wildly fluctuating state. This routine, for the most part, eliminates contemplation of their life as a whole together with the burden of struggling with everyday reality. Such a life-style has the effect of reducing consciousness of conflict and the need to make difficult decisions. Awareness of pain, disappointment and the impossible complexities of an inhospitable environment is largely removed. Destruction of the functioning of consciousness is on a continuum with other forms of self-destruction, with suicide at the extreme.

The function of consciousness

There is much discussion about the nature of consciousness, its function and purpose. It is the area of the mind where evaluation of experience takes place and where consideration can be given to possible consequences of further action. Such activity is geared to the satisfaction of biological drives. Having the capacity to consciously evaluate at least some aspects of a complex situation increases the possibility of finding a satisfying course of action. It seems to me that this capacity is closely associated with the degree of integration or wholeness.

Mary Midgley (1994), a moral philosopher, says that human self-consciousness makes us aware of our conflicting interests and forces us to make a choice. Awareness of such decisions gives rise to morals and ethical considerations.

She points out that this capacity to make choices about how to behave, which we continually exercise during our daily lives, distinguishes us from other animals. They appear to have a more instinctual way of responding. She also postulates that it is the conscious awareness of conflict which gives rise to a sense of freedom. It does not lessen conflict. Indeed, awareness of internal conflict about how to act is the source of a sense of freedom. There is awareness of several possible courses of action and the consequent choice of action. Is this the main function of consciousness? Socially established rules and moral considerations may influence the decision-making process alongside other conflicting demands, both internal and external. These ideas are close to the ideas of Eric Fromm, discussed in Chapter 8.

Very close to such ideas about consciousness is the term 'centre of gravity'. One of the basic ideas of psychoanalysis is to increase the consciousness of impulses which were previously unacknowledged. The existence of a dynamic mechanism (consciousness) means that ideas about possible actions may be brought together and manipulated in thought. This may make it possible to settle conflict about which impulse to follow. The drift towards unproductive or chaotic behaviour may be lessened.

Is consciousness of conflict possible for people whose internal world lacks cohesion?

At different times during life an individual may find it difficult to exercise the freedom of making a choice between different courses of action. The decision about which impulse to follow may be partly influenced by some kind of moral principle. Erratic and unpredictable behaviour is thought of as being typical of the adolescent state, when the whole being is in a state of flux due to the need to adjust to physiological changes.

> This phenomenon, the continual shifting of the centre of gravity of the sense of identity, produces the characteristic quality of emotional instability seen in adolescence and since it is based on the underlying splitting processes, the varying states of mind are in very little contact with one another. Hence the adolescent's gross incapacity to fulfil commitments to others, to carry through resolutions of his own or to comprehend why he cannot be entrusted with responsibilities of an adult nature. (Meltzer 1973, p.51)

This 'adolescent' frame of mind is not a matter of chronological age – a man of fifty years can exhibit such behaviour (Meltzer 1973, p.51).

When an individual, child or adult, is unable to cope within the constraints placed upon him, restoration of internal balance may be helped by exploration in psychotherapy. But, in the case of a child, it is necessary for the therapist to make sure that the family setting is, as far as possible, currently supportive of that child. Also, the chance of good results is made more difficult if the family pattern is itself formed on the basis of relationships between part objects rather than whole objects. A proportion of children referred for help belong to families which do not function on the general principal of respect for the individual. One or more of the conditions identified as being detrimental to development may be present. The existence of such complex relationships within the family has been an important consideration leading to the development of family therapy.

The symbolism of roads

In religious writing, roads, or ideas about finding a route through to a better life, are frequently used as a metaphor for the complexity faced by an individual in trying to organise his behaviour in a complex society, according to a set of principles, rather than being blown hither and thither like a Will-o'-the Wisp. John Bunyan (1965) outlines how a poor man manages, with much travail, to find 'the way' through to eternal life. The awful turmoil of conflicting imperatives suffered by Christian is depicted in such a way that he conjures up in words such situations as 'The Slough of Despond' and 'The Hill of Difficulty'.

Bunyan struggles with the language at his command and evolved 'forms suitable for the expression of his inner experience.' (Sharrock 1968, p.54) He felt it necessary to write an 'Apology' on account of the concrete form of his writing. Perhaps this need was a legacy of the many years of remorseless destruction of the visual arts which followed the reformation. The following is one verse from 'The Author's Apology For His Book', a long poem which prefaces his story of Christian's journey:

> Be not too forward therefore to conclude
> That I want solidness, that I am rude;
> All things solid in show not solid be;
> All things in parables, despise not we,
> Lest thing most hurtful lightly we receive;
> All things that good are, of our souls bereave.
>
> My dark and cloudy words they do but hold
> The truth, as cabinets enclose the gold. (1965, p.6)

Brian Masters (1985), biographer, embarked on the research necessary to write about the life of mass murderer Denis Nilsen. In one of his letters to Masters, Nilsen said of himself that he was 'an amoral John Bunyan moving backwards in all directions.' He also wrote about the extremes within himself and of the actions he knows himself to be capable of. At the times of the murders, a 'black persona' took over. His dog reacted by cowering out of the way. Nilsen's own father had deserted the family very early. Nilsen had a close attachment to his maternal grandfather, whose dead body was recovered from the sea after his fishing boat was wrecked.

Nilsen's introspection about his crimes, including a description of his feeling of being in total control, has already been mentioned. It is interesting that he equated his amoral acts with movement backwards. He was indeed drawn towards darkness and death. These ideas have something in common with children's ideas about sinking sand and of being sucked down, etc.

The life of Nilsen was well researched by Masters but it seems that there is vital information missing, probably of abuse, to account for the gross perversion of the forward movement. Judging by the extremity of his actions – the murders – it is as if when two people are closely connected, one is eliminated.

Many images produced in therapy bear a striking resemblance to the physical situations faced by Pilgrim in *Pilgrim's Progress* during his struggle to resolve conflict and move forwards. When roads begin to appear in worlds during a course of psychotherapy they usually represent the conscious search for direction in life. Their appearance often confirms that some advance in personal development has been achieved.

Ideas about travelling often occur in Worlds made by older children and reveal this search for direction. The following account shows how blocks impeding active participation in school life were removed when conflict over separation from parents was resolved.

Kate: Conflict is symbolised by two conflicting directions, one cutting across the other

The clinical material, described below, is from the case of a fourteen-year-old girl called Kate, referred for treatment for school refusal. It shows how the conflict over direction, related to the need for separation from her parents, was worked on and resolved. This case is different from some mentioned above because Kate's patents were supportive. Her personality was on the way to becoming well-rounded and her approach to life was, essentially, positive.

Kate had already been out of school for one year at the time of referral. She and her parents were extremely anxious. The social history revealed that a baby boy had died before Kate was born. When Kate was three years old she had an operation to remove a cyst from the thyroid gland. This must have intensified the normal anxiety of the elderly parents, who worried generally about health and were very protective.

Kate was practised at verbally denying the problem over separating from her parents. In earlier treatment attempts it had proved to be very difficult to make progress by purely verbal means. She was adept at rationalising her difficulties. But, when given the freedom to express her conflict in spatial terms using worlds, her progress was impressive. One day she made a world in dry sand, 'an exotic plant', with fencing to represent the pot. The plant was clearly 'pot bound' – the roots thirsty for a different kind of food, analogous to the 'food' that she needed from school. The message in the drawing contradicted her practised verbal denials about the need (and wish) to go back to school. She was also able to externalise her predicament by using the Lowenfeld World Technique.

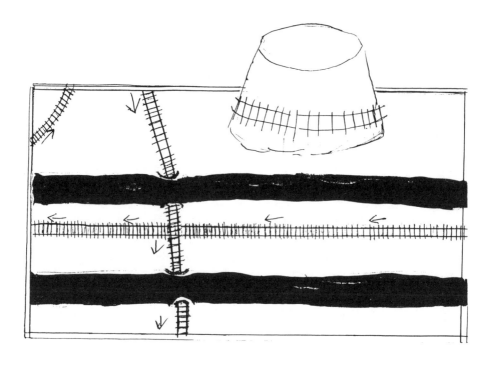

Figure 5.5: World in damp sand made by Kate aged 13 years

This was one of the first worlds Kate made. Two single rail tracks cut across each other. A menacing gasometer is at the side.

The two Worlds made by Kate

Example 1

This was, in fact, a railway layout. First, Kate made a single track between high banks. About half-way along this track she cut out holes in the banks and put in a second track cutting across the first. At the side of the track she made a large mound. It was a gas holder. These are bulky, rather threatening objects which can swell upwards from the lower position. The cross, formed by the two tracks at right angles to each other, represented her conflict over moving out into the world normally (also see the cruciform Mosaic – Figure 1.3, p.33 – made by Keith when he was beginning to face up to inevitable conflict). The large gas holder represented either the anxious parents themselves or her fear of upsetting them (at around the age of five she had ventured out on a tricycle. She ran it into the back of a parked car, hurting her finger slightly. The cycle was taken away from her and she was given a garden swing instead).

Figure 5.6: World in damp sand made by Kate

This was made six months after that shown in Fig. 6.5 just before she returned to school. 'The army is making sure the roads are kept open'. A final barrier to movement – top right-hand corner – was removed at the end of the session.

Example 2

The second World, a road system, was made about six months later, just before she returned to school. It appeared to be an ordinary road system except that the army had been called in to make sure that the roads were kept open. Several soldiers were holding guns. One was using a mine detector. Also, in the far-right-hand corner of the World picture was a level crossing closed off by a gate. Kate removed this gate just before she finished the session.

The contrast between the two lay outs is striking. The first World – two rigid tracks cutting across each other – was a cross formation representing the difficulty she had in satisfying her own wishes in the face of her parent's over-anxious protective restrictions. In other words, it represented her own conflict about moving away from home. The second World – an open system of roads allowing a free flow of traffic – revealed the good use she had made of the opportunity to explore her own predicament and to find a way forward. She made a successful return to school. Kate herself was a strong character whose parents, though over-anxious, were genuinely caring.

Confusion about direction expressed in the form of a maze

Rules and regulations, as well as moral considerations, are bound up with all human interaction. Mazes are often used, particularly by adolescent children, to represent the daunting and conflicting experiences of growing up in a complex society.

A sketch of a lively maze, set out using the Lowenfeld World material, by Kalyani, a fifteen-year-old girl, is included (she had earlier in treatment represented a church graveyard in a World described in Chapter 2). Kalyani belonged to an immigrant family, which meant that conflicting cultural demands added to her difficulties.

Painful infantile experience causes energy to be directed inward and downward away from reality and, perhaps, into passivity. Case material presented earlier, produced by James and Peter, illustrates this tendency to show energy moving downwards. Sometimes the act of objectifying feelings within therapy may be sufficiently powerful to activate a return to healthier emotional growth. Over time, the direction of movement, expressed within sessions, may be seen to change. Instead of being predominantly 'boxed-in', 'submerged' or 'down', there is movement forward or, something like growth, upwards and towards the light. This kind of change shows up in the patterns produced in drawings, 'Worlds' or Mosaics.

The Maze

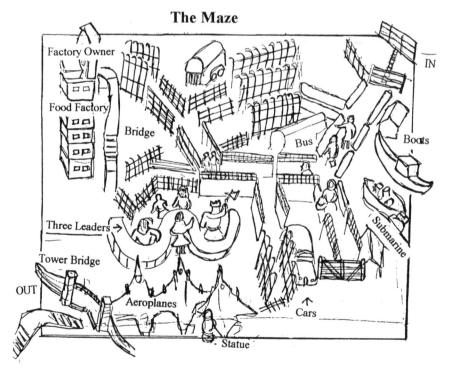

Figure 5.7: World in damp sand made by Kalyani

Figure 5.8: Mosaic made by Dora early in treatment

The boxed-in pattern gives a clear impression that energy was being used to hold something down.

Figure 5.9: Mosaic made by Dora towards the end of treatment

This gives an impression of an upward growing movement.

The two Mosaics produced by Dora (discussed earlier in Chapter 2), one at the beginning of treatment and the other towards the end, are a good illustration of how implied movement changes direction. The earlier pattern used only a narrow band of tiles near the lower part of the tray. These pieces were 'boxed in' above with black mosaic pieces, giving a clear impression that energy was being used to hold something down. The second pattern made by Dora illustrated an 'opening up' phase. It gives the impression of an upward, growing movement. Its production by Dora coincided with her readiness to return to school.

CHAPTER 6

Energy, power and access to resources

Gravity exists as an all-pervasive downward force against which we have to work. In the sense that accommodating to it demands an unremitting expenditure of effort, it is felt to be a negative force. The other main source of energy – the sun – is experienced predominantly as a benevolent source of useful energy. The sun provides light, warms us and we appreciate that it is essential for all forms of life, to make crops grow, and so forth (indeed, a certain amount of light seems to be necessary for our sense of well-being; shortage of it produces depression in some people).

Our experience of these two powerful sources of energy – gravity and the sun – places them, in some respects, in opposition to each other. The former demands a lot of effort accommodating to it, whilst the latter freely supplies energy in various forms. This ties in with our use of the up/down axis to evaluate experience. Being 'high' or 'uplifted' is associated with light and power, even with spiritual enlightenment. Being really low is linked with darkness and being drained of power. 'Darkness' embraces the unknown and all kinds of irrationality and monsters. 'Light', having the connotation of spirituality, enlightenment and transcendence, means that Heaven is bound to be high up, whilst Hell is down low.

Counteracting the pull of gravity, whilst becoming mobile and learning to walk upright, is a hazardous time for infants. Concentration upon awareness of the perpendicular and the need for balance in order to avoid being hurt expends a great deal of energy. Success in learning to cope with gravity is a big achievement for a small child. The emotional satisfaction involved is of a similar quality to that resulting from satisfying other basic needs through relationships. As Piaget points out, the infant adapts to his total environment without distinguishing between the various aspects of reality. Perhaps it is for this reason that position in relation to the vertical comes to be used as a yardstick for summing up the general emotional state, satisfactory or otherwise, according to whether or not current needs are being met.

The up/down axis, as a measure of power, is central to ideas about both the position of self in the concrete world and, used figuratively, about the structure of society

The capacity to structure wholes develops at the same time as learning to cope with gravity. The movement towards wholeness applies primarily to the self and also to objects that make up wider and wider reality. It progresses through the organisation of perceptions generated by satisfying and supportive interaction with others.

These two aspects of our internal structuring – awareness of power through countering the effects of gravity and the creation of a system of whole objects – are inextricably linked dimensions of our adaptation to reality whilst satisfying needs. The first symbolises individual strength and the second represents a state of relatedness. Indications about balance (or conflict) between these two dimensions may be deduced from behaviour and other forms of expression.

The tendency to be self-seeking, and the other tendency to enter into a mutual give-and-take, are, for most of the time, roughly in balance. When they are judged to be so, within a particular person's character, the summing up is likely to be that the person is 'well balanced'. At its best, normal self-interest combines with a degree of altruism, co-operative effort and concern for the common good. In other words, the quality of wholeness is about being able to act decisively, but, at the same time, it entails moral considerations. It develops through trust in others and the gradual realisation that others are essentially like oneself. It does not rule out conflict. Indeed, being able to deal with conflict, which may be experienced internally or socially, is a sign of increasing maturity. A lot turns on how the conflict is dealt with. For the individual, there is the internal problem of deciding how to resolve anxiety and conflicting wishes. The same kind of problem occurs between people in families and in other social groupings.

In the course of development the individual struggles to achieve a sense of self which combines with a working relationship with those around him. Each infant is dependent on a continuous flow of supplies, gained through interaction with those who create his environment. During the developmental process each individual builds up a unique system of knowledge based on his experience of these negotiations. This dynamic complex of ideas is developed in order to solve problems of survival. Directly or indirectly, it is concerned with energy (derived from supplies) and its physical source. Such ideas are bound up with the imperatives of life and growth.

Power, in terms of an ability to gain access to resources, is vital for any living being. Death is the alternative

I have in mind two main forms of resource which we need throughout life. Thinking primarily of the dependant infant, there is the purely physical form of supplies which provides comfort and nourishment. More difficult to define is the complex matter of the emotional support in the form of relatedness, provided primarily by parents supported by a social network. The nature of this emotional support is in the quality of relationships. It needs to include respect, continuity and setting of limits.

This second form of supplies is a product of the total environment. Of course, the quality of parental care is of crucial importance, but this is affected by the family's relationship to the society in which they are embedded. The conditions under which families are created and develop has a big influence on the way in which the offspring develop. The way in which the parents relate to each other influences the formation of the infants inner world. There is a balance to be struck between the urge to 'stick up for yourself' and the more all-round, reflective understanding of interdependency. Unfortunately, the members of some families function mainly at a level of part-objects. Inappropriate needs may be satisfied by adults with little respect for others.

Infants and children whose access to both kinds of supplies is very hazardous and, perhaps, painful are likely to have greater difficulty in developing skills of adaptation to reality. Their sense of self is likely to be more shaky because it has been difficult for them to develop a sense of their own efficacy. Trust in others, which depends on their being reasonably solid dependable figures who have your well-being at heart, is likely to be damaged by discontinuity in relationships, if not by outright neglect or abuse.

Some children, described earlier, were rejected to some degree by their mothers, for varying reasons. From the beginning of their lives, Jackie, Faiza and Daniel were in this category, though their situations were very different. Other children feel themselves in danger of being swallowed up, taken over and in other ways treated inappropriately because their individuality was not respected. Peter, Diana and Christine suffered degrees of over-impingement from parent or parents, who either abused or made great emotional demands on them.

A reasonably benevolent upbringing is likely to foster a capacity to 'stand on your own feet', deriving from an adequate level of integration within the self. Energies may then be directed positively, with a degree of consistency. At the other extreme, a nurturing situation which is characterised by severe discontinuity in the supply of resources, or which inflicts psychic pain, is likely to produce individuals whose inner lives, by definition, have never been contained or made whole. This means that much internal structuring, in the form of making connections which create wholes, has not been achieved. This condition is difficult to correct later.

Instead of a system of whole objects, what remains internally are fragments, many of them painful. This lack of connectedness stunts the emotional growth process. It renders purposeful behaviour all but impossible. This evidence points to the fact that emotional development and the capacity to think effectively are fully integrated aspects of the whole growth process.

The creation of wholeness within the child requires prolonged effort from parents, underpinned by help from the wider group. For this reason it is reasonable to suggest that a society that co-operates to provide support for those caring for children is likely to benefit in the long term in the form of a supply of capable young adults. The converse is also likely to be true: to allow children to be reared in run-down deprived areas is likely to endanger their development and present problems for society at a later date. If this kind of breakdown occurs, it seems to be a natural reaction for splitting to take place. The 'healthy' powerful part of society disowns the 'bad' part and takes up a punitive attitude. Those who try to take a more liberal approach are called 'soft'. The process of social splitting is under way.

The process of individual integration, of drawing a network of experiential information in towards the central area of focus accessible to thought, is essential in the development of a strong sense of self. Different aspects of experience which are accessible to consciousness may then be manipulated in thought. This increases the capacity to respond successfully. The 'highs' and 'lows' of experience tend to be softened and brought into a state of equilibrium. Good and bad may come to be seen as aspects of a larger whole.

A hierarchy of power within family or society works well, provided there is a degree of fairness and respect for the individual in both directions. This shared respect for the individual indicates that certain moral attitudes are shared and the society retains wholeness. But, in social situations where one individual, or group of individuals, is able to dominate and dictate the course of action against the interests and wishes of other members of the group, this situation is abusive.

Power and morality are inseparable. Both are involved in all aspects of human interaction. An egalitarian relationship between individuals means that each feels the constraints of the other's wishes. They experience a feeling of being 'on the same level', even if some have a degree of authority over others.

In the give and take between individuals, each makes demands on the other. Whilst transactions take place, by and large, to their mutual satisfaction, all goes well. But where one side makes demands that the other is unable or unwilling to meet, placing them in a position of stress or deprivation, the situation becomes volatile. This happens when abuse of power takes the place of respect for the individual.

In the early days of psychoanalysis Freud formulated his theories and placed emphasis upon the sexual roots of neurosis, to the exclusion of other factors. The central idea for Adler was the individual striving to overcome feelings of weakness in order to become strong and powerful. He began working on his own theories alongside Freud. But this state of affairs could not continue.

> Adler began seriously to differ with Freud and broke with the movement in 1910 to found a system based on the thesis that human behaviour can be explained in terms of a struggle for power in order to overcome feelings of mental or physical inferiority, and this system, whatever its status today, carried three implications which proved to be of the greatest possible importance to psychoanalysis and were finally, in one form or another, adopted by it: That neurosis was a disorder of the total personality, that the ego played a large part in its genesis, and that non-sexual factors could also lead to conflict. (Brown 1961, p.26)

In more recent years, the importance of power in all relationships has forced itself into our attention. The rights of the individual, gender issues and the drive for sexual and racial equality are being debated. The prevalence of the abuse of power in many different contexts is now being faced up to rather than being covered up and denied.

Only recently has it become possible to accept that the abuse of children occurs in some apparently normal institutions and families. Therapists working at the level of personal understanding may be confronted with evidence of the impact of such negative forces on the process of individual integration. The effect of such impingements is one of the main focuses of this book.

Damage to personal integrity is more likely to happen where suffering was uncontained, if the experience of pain and helplessness was not mitigated by comfort and solace from another human being.

Powerlessness, that is, being deprived of resources

Powerlessness is sometimes represented by images of objects being blown hither and thither in the wind. The wind, an external source of energy, moves the objects around randomly. A depressive quality often accompanies such images. A man who had been brought up in a children's home, who had never been able to derive strength from support and close relationships provided by a family, said that he always felt like a piece of flotsam, compared to people who belonged to families. He was expressing in spatial terms his feelings of emptiness and worthlessness about being cut off from the second form of supplies: loving support. I think that most forms of depression result from experiences of being severed from those resources which nourish the human spirit, derived mainly from creative relationships with others. The chemical changes within the body of someone suffering from a depressed state are likely to have been triggered by overwhelming and prolonged stress.

Ideas about power, energy and resources frequently appear in many different forms in play sequences. Often, the focus of this concern is anxiety about access to the source of supplies. Such anxieties are likely to originate in infancy, at the oral level, when the vital need is for milk combined with loving care. A child experiencing extreme privation and distress at the oral phase constructs a fragmented image, one with a totally different configuration from that created by a successful feeding situation. Positive feelings of value, with power to create a centre of gravity, are in short supply. The internal world is likely to be a loose grouping of part-objects incapable of being manipulated successfully in the imagination. Subsequent actions tend to cause further deterioration in relationships.

The feeding situation is sometimes represented in volcanic terms – as it was by Daniel, who also drew the unscalable mountain mentioned in Chapter 1. He drew a picture of a volcano, representing experiences originating at the oral phase, showing a little man landing on a round mound thinking that if he kept very still, it would be a safe place to land.

It turned out to be an exploding volcano which burned up a tree nearby and badly injured the little man, who was bleeding. Clearly, Daniel had suffered fear of annihilation from the maternal source of power. Overwhelming power was experienced as being external to the self. There appeared to be no sharing of power by mother and infant. Access to the vital supplies was fraught with danger. The perception of mother as a threatening figure continued through infancy – so much so that Daniel chose to remain in his own bedroom for most of the time when he was at home.

In all kinds of self-expression there is a complex of ideas associated with energy and its source, coupled with movement and its direction. These ideas appear in a wide variety of forms in Worlds, drawings, dramatisation, etc. A perennial topic is about success or otherwise in gaining access to supplies. Jackie's play (Chapter 4), particularly at the start of treatment, was about being down and being hurt. When one remembers that her repeated experiences of feeling hungry were first met with treatment for sore skin and hearing her own screaming, the pictures she made of crashing and being hurt make sense. At the same time, her main experience was of powerlessness. In therapy she began to bring into focus feelings of desolation and accept them as her own. As a child she still retained the capacity to grow, particularly in a situation where there was a sense of relatedness. The self strengthened and lifted slightly.

The self needs and strives to become an active agent in a position to deal with inevitable conflict and to make choices – provided the social situation allows it. Individualistic versus social demands may pull in different directions. The relative power of these tendencies gives shape to the personality, to some extent reflecting the values of society.

From a subjective point of view, one is active or passive in any particular situation. In social life an individual's experience of being active is in terms of the part he plays in any interaction and in the management of his own affairs. Is he able to live in a way that feels satisfying and appropriate or is his daily life a matter of submitting passively to the actions of others, regardless of his own wishes? One way of describing this latter situation is to say that the dominant energy or power comes from outside the self and is oppressive to the individual.

There has been a mistaken tendency to equate active and masculine, passive and feminine:

> There is also a tendency to assume that mothers are active while their infants are passive, this despite the fact that both suckling and sucking involve activity. In both instances formulations in terms of active and passive roles assume that relationships are collisions rather than interactions and confuse activity with initiation of action and passivity with responsiveness and receptiveness. (Rycroft 1968a, p.2)

A way of evaluating social interactions is in terms of the degree of discrepancy of power. To what extent do both sides have the capacity to influence events – or is the chance to be an active agent on one side only? Participants sum up the outcome of any social struggle in terms of their position in relation to the vertical – higher up (elated) or lower down (a depressive quality).

Being the winner in competitive situations brings the reward of feeling energised (on top) by being powerful, closer to the source of supplies, whilst the loser feels 'put down'. Success often leads to further success and increased room to manoeuvre – greater choice of action.

If during early life there has been the trauma of pain, hunger or emotional deprivation or of other forms of abuse, the healthy sense of personal power (efficacy) is damaged. The experience of being able to initiate progressive action to satisfy needs is frustrated. Trust in others is diminished and a feeling of emptiness ensues.

Without the containment of 'good-enough' parenting to supply attention and care, the internal world remains unintegrated – reflecting the condition of unresolved or extreme conflict within the social situation. Under such conditions consciousness likewise remains fragmented and depleted, in no condition to provide scope for thought and decision making. The individual is at the mercy of competing impulsive needs. Energy is expended chaotically – often destructively. The possibility of moral or social considerations being brought into focus and used to influence action is small.

Guntrip (1968) discusses the difficulty in differentiating between mental illness and moral failure pure and simple:

> Mental illness springs specifically from the ravages of early fear and the basic weakness of the ego, with consequent inability to cope with life in any other than a dangerous state of anxiety. Ideally, immoral behaviour occurs in a reasonably stable individual whose early education has given him bad values and standards of behaviour, or whose later experiences in life have caused in him a deterioration of the sense of responsibility to others and a drift into merely self regarding habits of mind. He is not necessarily a person undermined by deep seated fears. Yet we have to recognise that all to often, immaturity of development and deep-seated fears are hidden and defended against by the adoption of immoral, and even criminal ways of living. (p.11)

Guntrip quotes Winnicott's view that it is useless to attempt to inculcate 'tenets to believe in' if the child has not grown 'the capacity to believe in' through trust in human love:

> We have seen how too early and too intense fear and anxiety in an infant who is faced with an environment that he cannot cope with and does not feel nourished by, sets up a retreat from outer reality, and distorts ego-growth by a powerful drive to withdrawal and passivity. (p.87)

Drawing on case material, Guntrip illustrates the various forms that passivity and withdrawal from engagement in the real world can take. He talks of a withdrawal of the libidinal ego from the outside world so that the energy 'flows backwards' to infantile levels and 'downwards' into the depths of the unconscious. He describes how an individual withdraws from engagement in the outside world after having been faced with an environment he could not cope with and did not feel nourished by. Sometimes, possibly when therapeutic intervention has helped to marshal inner resources, it is interesting to observe that the direction of the flow of energy changes. It is then likely to be used more positively or creatively.

In her paper *Portrait of the Underdog*, Genevieve Knupfer says that:

...the lack of financial reserves prevents people from taking advantage of the few opportunities for making more money which do present themselves; the people who need it least have friends who can lend them money in an emergency. Moreover, the economic restrictions, because of the accompanying lack of education and perhaps a certain adaptation to submission and failure result in psychological restrictions which reinforce the economic. (Bendix and Lipset 1956, p.255)

The paper presents evidence to show that closely linked with economic underprivilege is psychological underprivilege – habits of submission, little access to sources of information, lack of verbal facility.

A situation where there is a high level of unemployment and restricted access to resources of all kinds, including education and information, means that there is concentration on the problems of survival. The instinct to survive means that the symptom of depression may give way to acts of violence. Antisocial acts become a way of gaining access to resources and/or as an expression of raw power without the social constraints which involve feelings of reciprocity. Feelings of 'give and take' and mutual respect can only develop in an environment which is predominantly benevolent, where co-operation is practised.

Growth and movement, the primary activities of life, flow from the expenditure of energy from resources already acquired

In normal circumstances physical and psychological sense of direction go hand in hand. But, when the individual is overwhelmed by distress early in life, perhaps by pain and loss of contact with those supplying love and care or by abuse, integrity is disrupted. Examples in the previous chapter, particularly of distorted body image, show how the normal orientation can be destroyed by impingement.

The sensation of being unable to exert power threatens confidence. Insecurity about the source of supplies de-stabilises the sense of underlying support. During the nurturing stage reliable support is essential for the creation of a centre of gravity, which is at the core of wholeness.

In Chapter 1, examples were given of how feelings about the effects upon us of the force of gravity are transferred to the assessment of our experience of social relationships. Similarly, the nature of a young child's close contacts effects the ability to experience attachment and to perceive wholeness. The capacity to think clearly, which is based on the development of concepts of conservation and constancy, depends upon this development, that is, the internalised system of whole objects.

Socially organised withdrawal of resources which marginalises or excludes certain groups of individuals

Within societies the needs and wishes of some members may be ignored or marginalised. At the extreme is total exclusion, which may amount to death. There are numberless examples of people who are relegated to a place on the continuum between social marginalisation and exclusion. The most obvious and basic way in which a social group may demonstrate that a minority group has little value is by restricting their access to the whole range of biologically required supplies.

The following example shows how child-rearing practices serve a deep-rooted cultural bias against women and female babies. This bias must have evolved to give some biological advantage. Perhaps it serves to keep population growth down by reducing the number of females. Population growth is a problem which many societies deal with, each in their different way. But my interest here is the psychological effects upon the girl infants.

Facts taken from a survey carried out in 1990 by SAARC (The South Asian Association for Regional Co-operation), are used in the following summary.

In India it is traditional for the birth of a son to be regarded as a blessing, whilst a daughter is seen as a responsibility and a financial burden. For complex cultural and economic reasons a son is, in some cultures, seen as indispensable in family life. In such societies the low status of females is entrenched, particularly in rural populations.

For centuries in India various means were used to do away with baby girls. Though female babies are born stronger than males, within a month of birth the death rate of female babies tends to be much higher than that of males. Girl children get less priority with nutrition and health care and are breast fed less than the boys. It is stated that, in the state of Rajasthan, if a girl baby is born, the women withdraw behind their veils and wail.

The reduction in the numbers of female babies, particularly in poor families, is achieved in ways which we in the West regard as brutal. Girl babies are seen as a commodity in over-supply or, alternatively, a drain on resources. The arrival of amniocentesis test centres in rural areas of India threatens to create an imbalance in male/female numbers.

From my observation of those Asian families where there is culturally instilled bias against female babies, it seems that the wives become extremely anxious about fulfilling their role in producing male heirs. A sense of failure (and a tendency towards depression) accompanies the arrival of a female baby, particularly if it is the first child. No doubt there are strong biological advantages behind this bias. Within families subjected to such pressures, the effects causing concern were mainly on the women and girls.

The following brief case study describes the family background of a young girl whose birth followed the death of a newly born male child, which made the bias against girls even more intense for her. The spatial ideas produced in response to her particular cultural/social situation revealed the state of her internal world. Much of the expressive material produced by Faiza involved movement in the up/down dimension. This dimension is associated with the struggle for a sense of personal identity. It is also involved in distinctions between animate and inanimate, active versus passive, potent versus impotent. Things that rise up have inner strength or are capable of growing and, in various ways, show that they are alive. Faeces, rubbish (worthless matter) and dead things fall or are actively disposed of in some way. Such preoccupations were a measure of her insecurity, a direct outcome of cultural forces which devalued her very existence.

Faiza: a brief family history is followed by extracts from clinical notes

Faiza was referred for psychotherapy to the local child guidance centre when she was almost six years old. Of crucial importance, for the happiness of the whole family, was the sex of each offspring. Faiza's mother had given birth to eight children in about ten years. Faiza was the fourth child of the marriage and three babies had been born after her – all girls. The baby born before Faiza was a second son, but tragically he died at birth. After his death the parent's overpowering wish was for another son to provide a brother for the older son.

Four healthy girls were born after the loss; Faiza was the eldest. A frequently heard regret, from both mother and father, was: 'Now we only have one son, but we have five daughters!' Faiza's mother seemed particularly sad about this.

One reason given for referring Faiza for treatment was that there were difficulties in her relationship with her mother. She had also been unable to settle in nursery school and the staff there said that she made them feel uncomfortable. At the time of referral she was in primary school, where the teachers worried about her. The educational psychologist had found it impossible to test her. At home Faiza was said to speak only odd words. The question murmured was: 'Is she autistic?' There was a long history of feeding difficulties. At the age of nine months Faiza had been hospitalised for various tests because there was worry over her not eating, and so forth. Fear of injections and other medical procedures stayed with Faiza on leaving hospital.

Faiza's parents were caring and conscientious, but this was overlaid with the male bias and the caring had a strongly coercive thrust. The prolonged stresses within the family during the years when three more daughters were carried and delivered confirmed Faiza's marginal status. Faiza's experience of loving care had been minimal, mainly due to her mother's depression after losing a cherished baby boy. She also had the burden of looking after three more girl babies that she didn't really want.

Faiza attended for a series of sessions, accompanied by either her mother or her father. She had a way of deflecting remarks and questions addressed to her. Faiza's play was free and imaginative, a little frantic. Now and then her eye contact was good; she enjoyed having someone's close attention. She talked a great deal, but only in short phrases. From time to time she was very interested in looking through the window at aeroplanes passing over the house and at the birds flying.

During the session when mother brought Faiza she talked about the death of the baby boy during birth in hospital. Faiza appeared to take little notice of this conversation. But she found the toy pram straight away. It was a carry cot on a metal frame. Faiza removed the carry cot and balanced the baby doll precariously on two bars of the metal frame. She pushed it around and, of course, the doll fell off – several times – through lack of support. She said that the baby was 'asleep'. And, in answer to my question 'Is the baby a boy or a girl?', she just muttered 'girl, boy'.

She later found an Action Man doll, pushed him head first into damp sand and began heaping damp sand on top of him, saying 'Eat! Eat!' She pushed food at him with a spoon (I later learned that both mother and father had been so concerned with her not eating that they had forcibly made her eat.) Then Faiza brought the Action Man into a standing position and made him shoot upwards. Her mother commented: 'She plays like a boy'.

Faiza was brought by her father several times. She was affectionate towards him with kisses. He was very involved in all aspects of her development, teaching her to count, and so forth, in a forceful manner. He was pleased to report that she seemed more outgoing.

He disarmingly told me what he did if she was not responsive: he took her little dolls (ones she made a great fuss of and took to bed with her) and put them in the waste-paper bin. He reported, with amusement, that she did not react to this immediately. She waited until his attention was elsewhere before retrieving them from the bin. Of course, having her precious dolls treated in this way both hurt and confused her. It confirmed her own precarious position in the family. She was also angry and afraid, but had to suppress her true feelings. In a later session when father was present, Faiza started by playing with the baby doll. The word 'poo' made its appearance. This time the baby was falling because the pram was 'broken'. The words 'daddy poo' and 'baby poo' were used several times.

But, the way in which she made the man shoot up out of the sand tray, and her interest in the planes flying overhead, revealed a healthy underlying striving towards self-assertion. After several weeks there began to be a slight suggestion that she would soon be able to express her negative feelings towards her father. But, culturally, this was unlikely to have been acceptable behaviour.

The theme of falling was continued in various forms using the doll's house. The lavatory was found and every one of the dolls-house dolls used it. 'Flush Flush!' went the loo. All the food on plates was pushed into the house. Then, people first, and later small objects, were pushed downstairs. Masses of stuff fell downstairs. Many children were popped into the house through an upstairs window. One adult male figure was carried out 'dead'. Then a smaller figure was taken out in the same way. Chaos had been created within the house; food, faeces, babies, all falling down, some of them dead. I think it would be too simplistic to say that she actually thought she was made of poo. Faiza's play using the house conveyed a sense of inner distress, confusion and anger. She seemed to be expressing the pent-up rage of frustration because her access to love and acceptance had been totally messed up.

The emphasis on things falling helplessly or being pushed down was symptomatic of Faiza's sense of being cut off from the supplies she needed to confirm a sense of personal value. The chaos inside the house reflected her fragmented inner world and the depressed feelings which engulfed the family. Her sense of self was under threat mainly because she was female. This real threat to her individuality was impeding her emotional and intellectual development.

Positive or negative use of energy

Activity resulting from a person's own initiative is experienced as being positive. But, if it is in reaction to the domination of others, it is experienced as being negative. Feelings about the nature of one's involvement with others are bound up with the sense of self-worth. Suffering deprivation or domination within a close relationship disrupts the normal creative flow of energy. Energy may be turned inwards and used to attack the self and keep in check forbidden instinctual reactions, resulting in some form of anxiety or depression. The following case study is an example of inhibition of natural impulses resulting from a sense of deprivation of maternal attention.

Amy, aged about six-and-a-half years, was referred for psychotherapy because she had not spoken in school for about a year. She was said to talk quite freely at home. She told her mother that the children at school were noisy. She did not like 'noisy' children and, of course, she herself was 'very good' – in other words, quiet.

When Amy was almost a year old her mother had had another daughter. This baby had cried a great deal and, from Amy's point of view, her mother was suddenly very busy trying to cope with the new baby. She had little time and energy left for Amy.

During her weekly sessions Amy played happily but silently. After several months attendance for weekly sessions she still had not spoken to me, her therapist. The therapy room was large, with cupboards holding a wide range of play materials. One item was a box of marbles which were used mainly by boys, who enjoyed sending them rolling across the floor.

Amy found the box of marbles, looked at them, and then went to the bag of building bricks and collected a few of them. With the bricks she arranged a small rectangular enclosure (coffin shaped). Marbles were placed carefully inside, filling the space, where they were blocked in, unable to roll. Having made this strikingly simple but surprising statement, which I think was a surprise to us both, Amy still spoke not a word. I wondered aloud about what it was that the immobilised marbles might represent. Did they represent the words that she kept closed up inside her mouth and which she really wanted to throw around? Or were they like the other babies who made so much noise and who ought to be shut away? Or did the boxed-in marbles represent Amy's feelings as a baby when she suddenly felt the lack of her mother's loving care and attention?

Winnicott and Lowenfeld both saw self-revelation as the key to playing and hence also to therapy. It means that interpretation should be used sparingly. The fact that Amy was able to create this simple but powerful image was therapeutic in itself, as pointed out by Winnicott. Through it she made a clear statement about the nature of her feelings. Her own situation was expressed in graphic terms, available to be explored verbally. By her creative use of materials she was able to objectify her predicament and begin to work through her suppressed, confused feelings.

Two weeks later Amy chose to bring her sister to join in her sessions. They played well together and Amy said a few words for the first time in my presence. It was soon reported that she had begun talking at school. She became more outgoing and began to use her energy constructively.

Questions about the techniques of psychotherapy: objectifying through play and/or the use of the transference?

Amy's use of play materials in the therapeutic space is a good example of the supreme value of play in the creative process of psychotherapy. I think that Margaret Lowenfeld overstated her own very good case, in favour of play techniques, by being in total opposition to the use of the transference in therapy. In a similar way, other schools of thought, particularly Kleinian, overstate the importance of the transference to the exclusion of other factors, such as the value of play in itself as a creative, self-exploratory process.

> The Lowenfeld World technique 'allowed for the exploration of both the inner world of the child and, simultaneously or on other occasions, the nature of his or her relation to a particular social reality; the children were seen to be attempting, through play, both to find harmony within themselves and to locate themselves in the social world in which they were growing up.' (Davis and Urwin 1991, p.9)

Lowenfeld concentrated on searching for meaning from the point of view of the child currently producing symbolic material. She stressed the need to suppress pre-existing theoretical prejudices long enough to allow time and space for self-expression.

Children (and adults) are frequently capable of objectifying their feelings and ideas by using play materials. For example, using the Lowenfeld World material to make a World is a creative activity, the individual making it is totally engaged, physically, intellectually and emotionally. The presence of the therapist, taking a keen interest in whole creative act (which quite often is worked through in silence), intensifies the creative experience. Observations, or even questions, may be put into words by the therapist and links and possible insights offered. In addition, when a careful record is kept of all Worlds that are made, they can be referred back to from time to time. It is then possible to trends and movements in development.

Shortage of supplies is a subject that appears frequently in Worlds in different forms. Here are two examples, both made by adolescent girls, who were refusing to go to school. Both were working through the conflict and frustration about whether to stay at home or go to school. Interestingly, as they worked through their confused feelings, mainly about relationships at home, the idea that came to the fore in both cases was that supplies were running out at home. The feeling that they were missing something by being out of school began to prevail and both returned to school.

Kate, whose two Worlds containing roads were included at the end of Chapter 5, made a very unusual World in dry sand. It was an elaborate arrangement representing what she called 'A pot plant.' This was modified into 'An exotic plant.' The fact that Kate chose to use dry sand for the outline of the pot, and outlined this with fencing to represent the pot, created the impression of being fenced in. When I suggested that remaining at home made Kate feel 'pot bound', she agreed and also admitted that she was missing much that the school had to offer.

Figure 6.1: World made in dry sand by Kate aged 13 years

'A pot plant'. 'An exotic plant'. Fencing was used to represent the pot.

The Market

empty

sold out

milk

empty

two figures looking
up at a lady selling milk

Figure 6.2: World made in dry sand by Kalyani aged 13 years

'A market'. 'It's a funny land'. All stalls are empty or running-out of supplies.

Kalyani, who made the graveyard in Chapter 1, made what she called 'The Market'. She said it was a funny land because all the market stalls, in the charge of round maternal figures, were empty or 'sold out'. Children were standing around asking for milk but were getting nothing. Kalyani was a less strong personality than Kate. She needed to start back in high school by using a unit designed to give support to children who could not cope straight away in the main school.

The place of the transference

At other times during treatment a child may transfer (or displace) feelings, ideas, and so forth which derive from previous figures in his life directly onto the therapist. When such transference occurs, once again insights are offered by the therapist. The case study of James in Chapter 2 illustrates the use of both approaches – objectifying through play and transference onto the therapist. Rycroft's (1968a) comments on therapy and what happens 'within the transference' is relevant here:

> Most accounts also assume that the therapeutic effects of analysis are largely due to the opportunity provided by it to resolve 'within the transference' conflicts dating from childhood and infancy, and attach little importance to the novel aspects of the analytic relationship, such as the encounter with a person who combines interest with non-possessiveness and whose insight into the patient is probably more articulate and possibly actually greater than that of the actual parents. (p.169)

When things are going well for an infant, having needs satisfied fairly soon after they arise is the dominant rhythm of their life. At this early stage the ease or difficulty with which access is gained to essentials has a pronounced effect on feelings of personal value. The nature of these early experiences has far-reaching effects on personal development. If an individual experiences power in these basic terms – that is, no great problem over access to the source of supplies – a sense of personal value is built up. This general sense of well-being – a 'centre of gravity' – forms a core around which the whole structure of self can begin to coalesce. To preserve the infant's early sense of wholeness, it is important that understanding of the limitation to this sense of power should develop gradually. At a later stage, learning to wait for things is an essential experience. Being able to wait in order to work towards objectives is achieved only gradually.

Difficulties in gaining access to supplies

Children in psychotherapy have experienced, almost certainly, above-average levels of difficulty over having needs met. At times of growing confidence, when some of these problems have been worked through in therapy, such children often like to assume the role of shopkeeper. By so doing they imagine themselves in charge of supplies. In fantasy this play turns the fear of shortages into its opposite: the enjoyment of being in control of boundless resources. There may be shops selling all kinds of provisions or farms set out in the sand tray growing crops or breeding pigs, cows, chickens, and so forth. Young animals (babies) of all kinds are perceived as being of great value.

A baby with a satisfying experience at the breast develops a sense of his own 'efficacy'. This term was used by Piaget to describe the embryonic sense of autonomy developing in such an infant. Winnicott talks in terms of an early 'illusion of omnipotence' when the mother affords the infant the opportunity for 'the illusion that the breast is part of the infant'. He goes on to say that the mother later gently disillusions the infant, but that she will only succeed if at first she has given sufficient opportunity for illusion.

Both terms, 'efficacy' and 'illusion', have in common the idea that it is important for the infant to feel from the very beginning that he is predominantly an active agent in achieving satisfaction for himself. Early feelings of omnipotence need to be respected and modified gradually, whilst trust in the accessibility of necessary supplies remains. Predominantly satisfying early experience creates the illusion that the infant is largely in control of his own affairs. This fosters the healthy sense of wholeness within the embryonic self.

The pressure on individuals generated by social flux and insecurity seems to be leading to an increase in behavioural problems in young people. The impoverishment of a large section of society produces one of the worst forms of abuse of children. Such neglect and deprivation is bound to increase the manufacture of delinquency and criminality.

Children within western countries are looked on, in relation to their need for resources, differently at different times and from two broadly contrasting points of view:

1. Competitive individualism is not compatible with the idea that all parts of society together form an interdependent whole; not 'all' the children are regarded as 'our' children. Those in power apply a split attitude to the nurture and education of the next generation; children, particularly those born to the least affluent members of society, are seen as a potential heavy drain on resources.

2. In contrast, a society which places emphasis on co-operation would look on all children, not just one's own, as being valuable and in need of nurturing. To give them a good chance of maturing into adulthood would be seen as an investment in the future of the society as well as the individual.

The provision of adequate resources to support those caring for infants and children would go some way towards reducing mental instability and the prevalence of antisocial behaviour. Such expenditure would benefit both individuals and society in the long term. The foresight required to ensure that adequate resources are provided for children's early years is often lacking.

Ensuing problems will require expensive measures which may or may not bring about solutions. If it is possible to take a long-term rather than a short-term view, we might discover the advantages of encouraging adequate provision for the next generation.

CHAPTER 7

Gravity and Social Forces

When a state of 'relatedness' with other people is made difficult or impossible for an individual, the tension created causes unhappiness, even insanity. For that individual, gravity and negative social forces have become confluent and the sense of self is under threat.

Psychology and sociology are like the two sides of one coin. It is not possible to go far in considering the shape of the individual's internal world without thinking about social context. Social interaction is concerned with the give and take of the full range of resources, tangible and intangible, used and created by humans. The character of each individual is greatly influenced by the manner in which access to these biologically required resources is organised. This largely determines the political structure of society in terms of control, social hierarchy and status. There is a political angle to all human relationships.

Erich Fromm (1955) writes about a certain point of animal evolution 'when action ceases to be essentially determined by instinct':

> When the animal transcends nature, when it transcends the purely passive role of the creature, when it becomes, biologically speaking, the most helpless animal, man is born. At this point, the animal has emancipated itself from nature by erect posture, the brain has grown far beyond what it was as the highest animal...what matters is that a new species arose, transcending nature, that life became aware of itself. (p.23)

Fromm looks on birth in the conventional sense as being the starting point of birth in the broader sense. He looks on the whole of an individuals life as being 'the process of giving birth to himself.' He adds that 'it is the tragic fate of most individuals to die before they are born.'

> ...After he has satisfied his animal needs, he is driven by his human needs. While his body tells him what to eat and avoid – his conscience ought to tell him which he needs to cultivate and satisfy, and which he needs to let wither

and starve out. But hunger and appetite are functions of the body with which man is born – conscience, while potentially present, requires the guidance of men and principles which develop only through the growth of culture. (1955, p.28)

Individual adjustment comes about through learning rather than instinct and is dependent on relationships within a particular culture. This process of individual development is made difficult by 'a constant and unavoidable disequilibrium' between what Fromm calls 'animal' needs and 'human' needs. When referring to human needs, Fromm is thinking about those attributes which distinguish man from animals, particularly the wish to transcend nature by creating a state of relatedness – even with the whole of creation. It is concerned with moral issues and a striving for wholeness and integrity.

Gravity and social forces together shape the internal world

The dichotomy that Fromm writes about, between 'animal needs' and 'human needs', has some similarity with the two dimensions of self-representations identified in an earlier chapter:

1. the up/down dimension related to power and gaining access to resources for energy and life,

2. the more all-round dimension which develops throughout life through relationships, leading to a degree of wholeness which is characterised by the need 'to unite with other living beings'.

Fromm (1955) says that 'to be related to others, is an imperative need on the fulfilment of which man's sanity depends.' (p.30) My own assumption is that when Fromm talks of sanity he is referring to the state of mind which is sufficiently whole to allow the dichotomy to function in a balanced way, a way we might have referred to at one time as 'civilized'. The two dimensions, related to satisfying animal and human needs, are often in a state of tension, sometimes amounting to conflict. Ideally, the dominant need is to be 'related' to other people.

The physical birth of a human baby is just the beginning of the process to create a human being

What is entailed when a family, supported by a community, sets out to rear a newborn infant? To bring a child up to a creative adulthood requires the expenditure of resources, particularly personal involvement, over many years.

It is during the years of infant dependency that basic attitudes are laid down. Being intimate with, and dependent on, others for a long period means that we learn about the relationship between weakness and strength, which is a fundamental aspect of family and social life. The give and take of human interaction is crucial for rearing a child who will, in turn, be capable of transcending the basic 'animal' condition.

In a reasonably just and equable society a balance is struck between individual needs and those of the wider group. There is a degree of respect both ways. A democratic society which has as an ideal respect for the individual would, of necessity, aim at distributing resources fairly. This principle, if acted upon, would re-create a sense of wholeness within the community. The effect would be to make child rearing less problematic.

For a society to be sufficiently cohesive and the various groupings to work together, individuals need to be able to make predictions about the behaviour of themselves and of others. Where there is reciprocity, and such power as exists is exercised with respect and moderation, interaction between individuals and groups is fruitful. There needs to be a fairly clear consensus about acceptable behaviour. Such a state of consensus appears to work well in a society like Japan. Though Japan has a steep hierarchy, the vast discrepancy in terms of distribution of resources in the USA would not be tolerated in Japan. There is also a strong belief in co-operative effort in the world of work, as opposed to directives being sent down from above. Widely shared traditions and value systems also make interaction in Japan more straightforward.

A working interaction between individuals within a society fosters an organic relationship between the patterns of internal and external worlds. The stability of functioning within the society depends on this correspondence. Socially creative interaction requires mutual respect and reciprocity. In an ideal world most of the members of the society need to be 'whole' individuals, capable of making allowances for the point of view of others. A reasonable balance between the interests of the individual and those of the wider group then becomes possible. But, this kind of balance within a society may be totally lacking.

Social forces at work shaping the individual members may be 'uplifting' for some and 'depressing' (literally) for others

To take an extreme example, the use of slaves releases those who benefit materially from physical drudgery. Those who gain freedom in this way then have time for all kinds of different pursuits, perhaps intellectual or 'spiritual'. The slaves experience little else but drudgery, but are not likely to be looked upon as being part of the society.

A statement made earlier in this book needs modifying. The purely physical world we live in is three-dimensional but events over time make our human world four-dimensional. Our reality, and the adaptation we individually make to it, evolves and is greatly influenced by history and culture. If the community we are born into has been impoverished over generations, our total lives, and consequently our inner world, is also affected.

The following poem is by the poet James Berry, describing an incident from his childhood in Jamaica. He witnesses his father being admonished by the young son of the plantation owner.

'A Schooled Fatherhood'

There in my small-boy years that day
couldn't believe the shock,
the blow undid me, seeing him abused,
reduced, suddenly. Helpless. without honour
without respect, he stood indistinct,
called 'boy' by the white child
in the parents' look-away, 'don't care' faces.
Lost, in a peculiar smile – being
an error, a denial of the man I copied,
that big man I'm one day to be – he made
a black history I didn't know swamp me,
hurt me, terror hands of a dreaded ghost.

Two men apart, from now – with him
not able to see, not able
to keep pace with time or know
my secret eye watchful –
I began to see
educated voices charging his guts
like invisible pellets of a gun
imbedding in him, daytime, night-time.
And soon, he clean forgot
who he was. Then with his roots
and person's rights wiped away
he knew he'd known nothing always,
His deep man-structure dismantled,
a tamed dog came in him and gave him face
gave him readiness for his job –
delivering shot birds between his teeth

to get a patting beside high boots –
my father

my first lord

my inviolable king. (Berry 1995)

James Berry's poem is particularly relevant to what I am trying to say because both aspects, the social/political and the psychological, are encapsulated in one expression.

Struggles over agency in social interaction

Andrew Samuels (1993) identifies two kinds of politics:

1. There is the organisation and distribution of resources and power within societies and between countries.

2. At an internal, personal level there is 'feeling level politics'.

But politics also refers to a crucial interplay between these two dimensions and between private and public dimensions of power. There are connections between economic power and power as expressed on an intimate, domestic level. Power is a process or network as much as a stable factor. This version of political power is demonstrated experientially: in family organization, gender and race relations, and in religious and artist assumptions as they affect the life of individuals (Samuels 1993, pp.3–4).

Samuels makes the point that 'the demarcation between the inner world of psychology and the outer world of politics has no permanent existence.' He also points out that 'feeling-level politics…reflects struggles over agency', meaning 'the ability to choose freely whether to act and what action to take in a given situation.' This is the crucial interplay between the public and private dimensions of power.

Though discrepancy of power exists in many social situations, it is the size of the discrepancy that is of crucial importance for the individuals involved. When James Berry (1995) writes about his father's situation, internal and external, he is describing a situation where transcendent needs, on both sides of the social divide, have been neglected.

In relation to the development of self, the crucial question is: to what extent do both sides have the capacity to influence events or is the chance to be an active agent on one side only? From the very beginning of life, these questions are important in the development of an autonomous self. Winnicott, in his understanding of the importance of the mother child relationship, emphasised the need for the infant's early feelings of omnipotence to be respected and for the infant's separation from this symbiotic attachment to be gradual. Sensitive handling of the infant means that the sense of trust is maintained and, in time, the infant is able to accept limitations to his powerful wishes, without damage to the infantile psyche.

Respect for the individual and the encouragement of a state of relatedness stem from a culture which values such attitudes as reciprocity and co-operation (it also must synchronise with the economic requirements). I realise that this is an idealised state of affairs, where discrepancy of power exists but is kept within bounds. The participants would certainly, in theory, be able to behave as whole human beings, their integrity having been respected. In this imaginary society the distribution of resources would be reasonably fair and, at least, adequate for parents to care for the young through prolonged dependency. It seems that where competition for scarce resources is kept to a minimum, relatedness is given greater emphasis. This is not the state of affairs that prevails in the burgeoning global market which is driven by fierce competition.

Society is able to take on an infinite variety of forms. The integrity of the individual, with which we are concerned, is, perhaps, a recently acquired cultural ideal. The aim of most people on this earth is to stay alive. Most societies are concerned with competing with each other for resources in order to survive as a group – or at least for the survival of those who are dominant within the group.

Many societies have a tendency to undergo a splitting process whereby certain groups, dominant within the society, are content with situations where other less powerful groups remain in a state of deprivation, separated off and, as far as possible, ignored. Heaping reward on the successful is rationalised, by those in power, in terms of their virtue, hard work and talent. Allowing the unsuccessful to fall becomes part of the logic.

A causal link must surely exist between the amount of unresolved conflict inside individuals and the amount of fragmentation and conflict within the society that nurtured them. A society characterised by intense individualism and competition plays down the need for interdependency and sharing. The very existence of 'society' as an entity is denied. Deep divisions within a society, combined with a gross imbalance of power, make it difficult to settle the perennial human conflict between satisfying self and respecting others. Fruitful interaction between sections becomes difficult. This split state is reflected within internal worlds. Even for well-placed individuals who have developed an awareness of the needs of other people, achieving a balance between what Fromm called 'the internal dichotomy' is made difficult because they have to comply with splits in operation.

The interplay between the public and private dimensions of power

Human beings have an innate need to live in groups. The way in which these groups are organised is infinitely variable. Our general feeling of satisfaction (or disappointment) is gained through personal effectiveness in social interaction. Events affecting families, groups and societies all have their impact on each individual.

Human reality is four-dimensional

The parents' behaviour towards offspring is, to a large extent, determined by their own developmental experience. They carry within them the history of their own adaptation to reality, fashioned by past events and conditions within their own family. Patterns of adaptations and relationships tend to be repeated, only evolving gradually.

The nature of relationships within the family and, in turn, the quality of interactions within the total social environment play a crucial role in developing the potential of the next generation (for the sake of simplicity, genetic variability is left out of account). Breakdown in access to those supplies, necessary for good adaptation to the real world, if severe, may cause stress and ill-health. If it occurs in early infancy, it disrupts the formation of a healthy, autonomous self. It may even start in train the formation of violent criminal traits.

In the early days of psychoanalysis, Adler expressed ideas about the individual's efforts to exert power in his own particular setting. Because of the unacceptability of these ideas at that time, they became detached from the main stream of Freudian theory. The following is a summary of Adler's position:

> Character, therefore, is regarded by Adler as an interlocking set of attitudes which has been adopted by the individual in order to deal with the types of situation to which he was exposed (e.g., his bodily constitution, his social and economic position, his sex, the family constellation and his position in the family, his education, and so on). The traits which he produces are adopted because of their functional value to him in the earliest years of life; they were traits which seemed to give him the best results in terms of power, in the particular setting in which he was placed. (Brown 1961, p.39)

Guidano (1987) links these individually created structures to general theories of knowledge as set out by Lorenz and Piaget. He says: 'The application of an evolutionary perspective to the growth of knowledge seems to reveal that knowledge itself – being the result of biological and adaptive processes – has evolved along with other aspects of life' (p.6). There follows a discussion about the relationship between self-knowledge and reality. Since knowledge is gained during the process of solving problems in the real world, and in an attempt to anticipate and control events, various theories are constructed. Such activity plays a central part in the behaviour of organisms. The construction of the inner world results from this kind of activity. This means that this world about which we continue to theorise is 'co-dependent with our experience, and not the ontological reality of which philosophers and scientists alike have dreamed.' Guidano goes on to say '…knowledge, being a theory of the environment to which the organism has adapted, always reflects the specific self-referent constraints through which the organism scaffolds his own reality.' (p.7).

So, if self-knowledge is formed through interaction with our total environment, our internal world is organically related to the particular conditions and constraints with which we have had to contend. For some, the constraints will be largely benign, whilst for others, problems associated with gaining access to the necessary supplies will have had adverse effects on all-round development. Of particular interest is the way in which individuals and groups accommodate to the needs and wishes of other people, particularly if such motivations conflict with their own.

Margaret Lowenfeld was very interested in the relationship between internal patterns and the characteristics of a particular way of life.

> Of all psychotherapeutic approaches, Lowenfeld's is perhaps one of the most explicitly socio-historical. Throughout her work she forefront the social and historical conjuncture in which her theories, presuppositions and approach were grounded. By implication, this historical location also applied to her child patients (Paris and Urwin 1991, p.11)

They continue:

> In the developmental necessity to find means for representing experience to the self, and expressing it, the human mind demands meanings from the culture in order to locate itself. These transactions thus have a constitutive effect on the developing psyche; they are not grafted on afterwards. (Davis and Urwin 1991, p.11)

How cultural influences become represented within the psyche in the form of a pattern is a very intriguing subject.

Two contrasting patterns representing societies

I came across the two following patterns, representing societies, quite by chance during the time when I was thinking about this book. They were verbal descriptions by individuals from two different countries at different historical times.

The first is by Victor Hugo in *Les Miserables* (1992). Though he was born into a prosperous, privileged section of France, he chose to identify with those less fortunately placed. A dominant theme of the novel is the quality of interaction between people. Some of Hugo's characters show a cavalier disregard about the effects of their actions on other people's lives. Hugo creates an image of society from the point of view of Jean Valjean, a man who is lodged in the bottom layer of the social pyramid:

> …he saw, with mingled rage and terror, forming, massing and mounting up our of view above him, with horrid escarpments, a kind of frightful accumulation of things, of laws, of prejudices, of men and of acts, the outline of which escaped him, the weight of which appalled him and which was no other than that prodigious pyramid that we call civilisation. (Hugo 1992, p.80)

Les Miserables has a strong moral, religious theme. The old priest, referred to by Hugo as "The upright man" (p.3), represents ideals of sharing, compassion and forgiveness. By his actions he kept these ideals, linked to feelings about social solidarity, alive. They may be regarded as too altruistic under the increasingly competitive conditions which exist today. Competition tends to be seen as the only possible way forward, although, at the same time, many people see the need for attention to be given to human rights.

The second example of a pattern representing society contrasts with the preceding one. In her published memoirs, Virginia Clinton Kelley, (1994) mother of President Clinton, describes her own strenuous conscious efforts to divide her inner world into good and bad. Central to this pattern is a strong, white, air-tight box which keeps safe inside it everything she holds dear – love, family and friends. All else, with negative associations, is kept outside the box, and is black. The formation of the divided inner world reflects the nature and history of social pressures on her as an individual.

Hot Springs, where Virginia spent most of her adult life, was a fast, exciting place. Its economy was largely dependent on racing, gambling and prostitution. Gangsters had been known to reside there. The main rule in operation was to enjoy yourself. A man was assessed in terms of how much money he had, no matter how he had acquired it. With money went power, and those who had it could get away with doing things other people could not get away with. The con-job was considered to be an art form.

Comparison between two social patterns

The patterns, one in the form of a pyramid, the other organised into two opposing areas, highlight two different value systems within the societies. The permeability between inner and outer worlds is also illustrated.

A bias towards wholeness, relatedness

In Victor Hugo's text, society is a strongly structured organic whole. For him, the quality of relationships between people is of the utmost importance. The social hierarchy is steep but there is an inherent belief in the absolute ideals of justice and the intrinsic value of each individual. In reality, life is very harsh for those without power. The tension between institutionalised power and the rights of all individuals is still being debated, and there is the hope that a balance will eventually be achieved. Respect for the individual and the importance of ethical dimensions of society was the dominant theme. Hugo was part of the political movement which had, as its ideals, liberty, equality and fraternity.

A bias towards individuality, divisiveness

The pattern produced by Mrs Kelly reflects the cultural pattern. The emphasis in the USA is firmly on competition. Polarities such as success and failure, good and bad, black and white (including race) dominate attitudes and thinking. The physical and psychological separation of those who have 'made it' from those who have not has become so wide and antagonistic that there is a threat to the society's capacity to function as a whole.

The emphasis on competition between individuals and groups tends to rule out institutionalised ways in which people can work together in a common cause. The debate about everyone's right to have access to necessary resources appears to have been lost in favour of the individual's right to accumulate power and those individuals who do accumulate power, usually in terms of wealth, are able to lead lives devoted to an extreme form of conservative individualism. Competitive individuality has been compounded with the individual's right to bear arms – a legacy of their pioneering history. Indiscriminate use of the handgun has further aggravated the situation. The gun has come to be thought of as indispensable and is, for many, a symbol of individual power.

In American cities the massive skyscrapers which tower over people symbolise the accumulated wealth of the corporate financial institutions and emphasise the smallness and weakness of the general mass of people. The proper interchange of ideas between ordinary people and between groups, necessary for a democracy to work, is minimal. The split between those with power and wealth and those who have none is virtually complete. In some areas it is true to say that a war is being waged between two opposing factions, generating fear and hate. Just as successful efforts to gain access to supplies creates a lift in the spirits, extreme difficulties in doing so gives rise to feelings of falling, of depression.

Recent research shows that winning and losing have a direct effect on the chemical composition of our brains, particularly on levels of a neurotransmitter called serotonin. Winning raises levels, losing lowers them. People with low status suffer from low serotonin levels. This tends to produce depression in women and violence in men. Findings suggest that the cause of these chemical changes is within the environment, not, as one might expect, in the genes. Both depression and violence are caused to a large extent by feelings of subordination arising from being made to feel like a loser within families and the wider society (James 1997).

Cultural marginalisation: the effects on personal development of being female and therefore classified as of less value

The cultural dominance of males over females produces advantages (and some disadvantages) for the society as a whole. But the case study of Faiza, described in the previous chapter, was mostly concerned with how cultural demands for boy babies, rather than girls, impacted on her individual development. Her birth did not bring forth affirmations of love and acceptance. In many subtle ways it was made clear that she was not what the family wanted. To be the cause of such overwhelming disappointment to her parents deprived her of that feeling of being encircled and supported which is the basis for the development of a strong sense of self. In her play the emphasis was on things falling helplessly or being pushed down.

Social deprivation and unemployment

> Shylock: 'You take my life, when you do take the means whereby I live.'
> (Shakespeare 1967, p.146)

Many workers lose their jobs and suffer loss of status and deprivation as a result of, what appears to be impersonal economic forces, enabling the economy to function more efficiently. A person experiencing such loss needs a robust sense of self to be able to survive intact and re-establish his position.

The long-term unemployed are, in effect, at the mercy of overwhelming outside forces. Competition fosr scarce jobs emphasises separateness, individuality and vulnerability. This process has had the effect of reducing social solidarity amongst the large group which was known in the past as 'the working class'. Groups of such people tend to be separated off, denigrated by the rest of society. They may be referred to as the underclass. They will be seen as a drain on resources by those established higher in the social order. Their own impotence, dejection or fear of further deprivation may be projected onto others who are in an even weaker position, or the aggression may be turned inwards against the self, sometimes causing depression.

Paul Martin (1997) writes about the vast complication of the immune system and the effect upon it of prolonged stress:

> For a start, unemployment can be very damaging to personal relationships and family life. The rates of divorce, domestic violence and child abuse are significantly higher among families affected by unemployment. Unemployed couples are twice as likely to divorce as couples where at least one partner has a job. The children of the unemployed have a greater risk of being taken into official care. Unemployment conspires to destroy people's social relationships at a time when they need them most. (p.186)

Family stress is almost bound to cause deterioration in child care. Ill-health or marital breakdown are often part of the whole picture. In extreme situations violence becomes a way of expressing frustration. For a large number of people in western society, particularly those at the bottom of the hierarchy, the possibility of finding a way of satisfying their own needs whilst complying with the codes of behaviour demanded by society has become extremely difficult. Internal and external resources are effectively depleted. It is hardly surprising that we find internally fragmented lives in deprived social settings, cut off from the legitimate mainstream of highly rewarding competitive activity.

Three children from the same deprived family were referred for treatment to child guidance centres

Where the inner world (reflecting the external world) is full of disorganised drives and sensations demanding instant gratification, the individual is blown hither and thither in an unstable world. There are social demands exerting a downward pressure. Paul and Katherine's family, briefly described below, were from such a family. Both appeared to have suffered abuse.

Paul was a vulnerable fourteen-year-old boy. He suffered from alopecia and was finding it very difficult to attend school regularly, where his attainments were poor. He was from a very deprived background with a high incidence of ill-health. He was clearly under a great deal of stress but he was unable to feel sufficient trust in the therapeutic situation to commit himself to attend for treatment after two diagnostic interviews (it may have been that he knew that there were conditions at home which he was afraid to discuss).

During the interviews he made statements which seemed to be made in order to give me the impression that everything was all right. A moment later, remarks slipped out which contradicted previous statements. Everything during Paul's initial interview pointed to the inability to move forward in a particular direction. He made a World in the sand tray – a farmyard scene. A road was part of this picture. This road doubled back on itself, ending up leaving the tray further back than where it had started.

In a similar manner, making a Mosaic, he could not settle on, or elaborate, any particular pattern. The arrangement of tiles changed continuously and erratically. He started with one kind of arrangement, then abruptly removed it to start something else. After attempting, for a long time, to make a pattern, he looked pale and appeared to be physically exhausted. There was no more time available. At this point the remaining tiles formed a black shape hanging from the further edge of the tray. It had a menacing quality. Inner turmoil appeared to be the cause of his inability to settle to any course of action.

Katherine was Paul's cousin and was referred at the age of eleven by her mother, who reported that she had been sexually interfered with by a stranger. At a later date mother reported a further incident, but this time she said that it had involved a grown-up cousin. At a later time during treatment Katherine produced a picture of a 'Catherine Wheel', which conveyed the sense of disorientation. Sexual assault would have had such an effect, being damaging to autonomy and integrity. As is common with children being referred for psychotherapy, Katherine had little understanding of time – another indication of her weak sense of self and restricted understanding of reality.

Katherine made a Mosaic which had projections moving inwards from each corner. The central area was empty. This pattern shows a denuded sense of self, together with power projecting in from the outside. It is a type of configuration which I have seen produced by two other girls, both of whom had violent older brothers. As has already been pointed out, Katherine was Paul's cousin. Some time later Katherine's older sister referred her own four-year-old daughter to the child guidance centre. She was the third member of the family to be referred.

The family to which Katherine and Paul belonged appeared to have a complex of problems which had social deprivation as a central cause. Such factors as unemployment, poverty, poor health and being of mixed race were factors which all played a part. In such adverse social environments, the whole situation seems to be characterised by a depressed sense of individual value, which pervades all relationships. Lack of respect for the integrity of each other

Figure 7.1: Mosaic made by Katherine aged 11 years

This pattern, with projections coming in from each corner and nothing centrally, indicates a denuded sense of self.

Figure 7.2: Mosaic made by Naomi aged 11 years

may develop into a complex of abuse. It has already been mentioned that individuals who suffer low social status, and all the accompanying deprivations, may become depressed or aggressive. Individuals in weaker positions are likely to be at risk.

For comparison, a Mosaic made by another adolescent girl named Naomi is included. She was from a middle-class family and she had a non-identical twin sister. She was a clever, rather quiet girl who had good reports from school. For some reason, which I did not understand, Naomi was disliked by her mother, whilst no complaints were made about her sister. Naomi made several Mosaics which all had very heavy, colourful patterning in the outer areas. This one had a well-constructed, black circular pattern in the centre.

The virtual exclusion of whole groups from the main stream of life

In societies where there is vast discrepancy in terms of power and access to resources between the top and the bottom of the hierarchy, wealth 'trickles down' only so far. Abuse goes all the way.

When terms such as 'divided' and 'fractured' are used about advanced western society, they are usually coupled with concern about the welfare of impoverished groups of people. Aside from moral implications, it seems to be realistic to feel anxiety about what the outcome might be of such neglect and exclusion. Social breakdown is likely to spring from stress induced by poverty when it is combined with awareness of gross inequality in the distribution of resources. Impoverishment is experienced both materially and in terms of personal value.

The poem by James Berry, printed above, about the destruction of his father's spirit by external power causes us to think about 'the crucial interplay between the public and private dimensions of power'. Though the events happened around 1930, several generations after slavery had been abolished, the crushing effect of past, and continuing, traumas, including economic and emotional subjugation, still dominated their inner lives. Virtually total power was still retained and exercised by 'whites' over 'blacks'.

We can only surmise about the inner lives of the whites. With the emphasis for them on exerting personal power over others, rather than submitting to it or accommodating with others, this would, of itself, represent a weakening of what Fromm would call the 'human' aspect of the self – in other words the capacity to relate with respect to others. The general shape of adaptation would be in favour of aggression, self-assertion and domination rather than relatedness. Also implanted would be the acceptability of a cleft in society.

I make no excuse for including a second poem by James Berry. Talking in abstractions about deprivation, abuse and deep divisions in society, one tends to be able to get away from the reality of human experience. In this poem we see the effects, at close range, of the human instruments of power on the lives of people virtually without power. It describes happenings more than eighty years after slaves were emancipated.

Notes on a Town on the Everglades 1945

Sounds of 'Ma Baby Gone'
make the ghetto air in blues
in this southern town.

It charges me with dread
with puzzlement with wonder
at this haunted mass of black people.

They hum the blues in shanty streets
and open fields. They dance the blues
in bars. They pray blues fashion.

They gesture and move and look
like refugees or campers on home ground,
or just a surplus of national propagation.

And fenced in, policed, blues ridden,
the people plant wounds
on any close body it seems.

Women and men, all ages, go and come
in bandaged movements
like hospital escapees.

And on the compelling side,
the gleaming nearness of town,
the bridge is policing.

White men through their streets,
like white men in the fields,
are knowing and proud stalwarts,

With cold eyes like passionless gods
their groomed bodies go
extended with guns.

(Berry 1995)

This is a chilling image of the confrontation between two groups of human beings, one group controlled by the other. The inner worlds of both sides, which still incorporated the divide which governed and separated them, had changed little since the days of slavery.

In discussing the creation of self, I have mostly been concerned about those who have been unsuccessful in their attempts to deal with reality. Predominantly, they have lacked autonomy, have been unable to find direction and were generally 'down'. Usually the difficulty has been created by the nature of their relationships, past and present. Winnicott and others emphasised the importance of the primary nurturing relationship. More and more it has come to be realised that such conditions as over-impingement, deprivation or outright abuse are involved in developmental breakdown. Environmental problems are also involved.

Therapists are confronted in their work with children and adults whose integrity has been damaged and who are unable to cope with conditions which beset them. Often, they are disorientated, confused and generally down. A complexity of internal and external forces has overwhelmed them. Sometimes, oppressive external forces are still in place and therapists are sometimes asked to collude with them and treat the 'patient'. At such times a wider view is needed. Family therapy may be a better point of departure but is fraught with difficulties.

The inner worlds of those in powerful social positions

This subject leads into an enormously wide subject, well outside the remit of this book. One body that is addressing itself to the study of the personalities of powerful figures is The Institute for Psychohistory. In broad terms, they ask questions about the state of the inner worlds of influential participants in social organisation, not those who have fallen by the wayside. In one volume of their journal on the subject of 'Psychotherapy of Society', there are papers on such topics as 'The deep structure of Conservative ideology' (p.289) and 'Dangerous Leaders' (p.331) (*The Journal of Psychohistory*).

Power, in the hands of a tyrant, is likely to multiply the potential for conflict between people because opportunities for interrelationship is reduced to a minimum. Tyranny reduces the opportunity for co-operation between people and is likely to create disruptive factions. A tyrant (often someone who has come up the hard way) is, by definition, someone who enjoys wielding power for its own sake. It may well be that having experienced extreme and prolonged threat to the self, the vulnerable individual is likely to feel impelled to exercise tyrannical power over others. The oscillation between weakness and power happens in the lives of insecure people. The two paintings made by Kevan

(Figures 1.8 and 1.9) illustrate this swing. The first picture is of the self overwhelmed, the second shows 'Mighty Me.'

Internal worlds are slow to develop and, with modification, are carried forward through generations. To make reparations for the traumas suffered by the blacks whose ancestors suffered slavery would take a great deal of effort over a long period of time by those willing and in a position to do so. I think that the society as a whole would need to make such restitution in order to attempt to heal the rift and regain the capacity to function as an organic whole.

'...the demarcation between the inner world of psychology and the outer world of politics has no permanent existence' (Andrew Samuels 1993, p.4)

Our world, being four-dimensional, means that past events are projected forward through family and social history via learned adaptations.

Marsha Hunt, a black American writer, grew up in a ghetto in Philadelphia. She revisited it and made a documentary film about how the modern black population are living. Though their forebears made a big contribution to the establishment of capitalism, they are still not accepted as American citizens by the white people as a whole. She said that it seems as if they are uninvited guests, with the rest of society wishing they would go away.

Most of the black population remain in the ghettos, separated off in a harsh, violent environment with insufficient effort being made to educate them. The deep separation from the time of slavery has not been dislodged from internal worlds. Verbal protestations about equality are one thing, but deeply held attitudes may be at variance with these ideals.

But, if a society is to avoid breaking up into warring factions, all need to accept the fact that members are interdependent, participating in a complex whole. Towards this end it seems to be a healthy sign when one section of society becomes capable of thinking about how other groups are faring. There needs to be time, place and the will for genuine democratic 'give and take' to flourish. Perhaps this will only be brought about when it is seen to have survival value for the whole group.

The concept of wholeness, or lack of wholeness, applies equally well to society as it does to the individual's internal world

The necessity to find ever-new solutions for the contradictions in his existence, to find ever higher forms of unity with nature, his fellowmen and himself, is the source of all psychic forces which motivate man, of all his passions, affects and anxieties. (Fromm 1955, p.25)

To restore or establish an organic wholeness within a society or an individual is the need to explore and bring into relationship disparate factions or impulses. In the long term, rifts within a society are just as untenable as within the individual psyche. In both cases, tension between different parts, if left unresolved, will erupt in more violent form. Suppression of individuals or of basic human impulses, which always entails making access to basic supplies difficult, does not work for long in either sphere. The will to survive is strong in all people, as is the urge for self-assertion.

Living in a society with deep divisions and maintaining wholeness internally is difficult in the extreme. Nadine Gordimer (1979) wrote about the tensions of her life in South Africa during Apartheid. The theme of her novel *Burger's Daughter* was the conflict between the desire to live a satisfying personal life and the rival claim of social responsibility towards those discriminated against on the basis of skin colour: 'This contradiction that split the very foundations of my life, that was making it impossible to see myself as a man amongst men.' (p.25)

Even where the emotionally mature person holds the two aspects – self interest versus the wider interest – in reasonable balance, a degree of tension and conflict is entailed. This is the universal human dilemma. Individuals vary a great deal in their capacity to take a wider view. But, in the last resort, the capacity of any of us to act morally is usually affected by an appraisal of our own well-being and our chances of physical survival. We cannot forget that individuals, and groups of individuals, are biologically primed to strive, and even to fight and kill, for their own and/or their group's survival. A survivor from a sinking ferryboat said that his view of life had completely changed. He had seen young men push others off ladders in order to escape the rising water. He said simply, 'Everyone wants to live and has the right to live'.

Where the internal world is reasonably well integrated there is a sense of freedom in relation to choice about action. But this becomes an unattainable paradigm when consciousness is depleted by rifts which render thought impossible and cause people to interact on the basis of part objects. Because of their co-dependency, internal and external rifts are likely to reflect each other in an organic way.

The need to settle differences over direction arises constantly as a consequence of the complexity of choice for both individuals and society. The freedom to bring ideas into the appropriate forum is the first step towards working out a resolution. The conscious airing of internal conflicts as they arise promotes flexibility of action and gradual adjustment. Conflicting wishes may be brought into focus, assessed in terms of consequences and manipulated in thought. In a similar way, when there is opportunity for the discussion of ideas within a community, decisions about courses of action are more likely to work in the long run.

A phenomenon from the history of Western democracy, the position of the 'forum' in the centre of the Roman city was a visible manifestation of the value placed on discussion and the exchange of ideas. Perhaps it is analogous to Winnicott's idea about the sharing of play space, particularly in psychotherapy, or even to the location of consciousness – inner space within the body. For the individual, the quality of the state of consciousness is of crucial importance because it is the forum where accessible ideas may be brought into focus for internal discussion. This is where 'value', in the emotional sense, is assessed. It is certainly not just a matter of logical deliberation. Where a reasonable level of wholeness develops through trust and relatedness, tension or conflict, when it arises, may be worked through and, to some degree, resolved.

Conclusion

Thinking about the use of the forum in early democracy is an appropriate place to end this discussion about gravity and the self. It salutary to remember that in those optimistic days, slaves were used in the background and large tracts of the earth remained unplundered, an apparently limitless source of supplies.

Appendix
A Piaget-type experiment to test shape constancy

This project was carried out in 1959 at Birkbeck College in London. The reason for including this piece of work here is that it threw up interesting questions. These centred on the reactions of one boy in particular who seemed to be teetering on the brink of achieving constancy of shape but could not stabilise superficially conflicting impressions. When I discussed my impression of his reactions with the head teacher, she remarked on the erratic behaviour of his mother. This raised the question of the role of the mother in fostering the unfolding of intelligence. Was his difficulty in stabilising basic concepts a result of his mother's instability and unpredictable behaviour? If so, the lack of regularity in his environment would then be reflected in his difficulties over forming concepts of conservation.

The child's conception of quantity represented by a two-dimensional shape

Abstract

The experiments were made in an attempt to establish that the conception of conservation of wholes of a simple type, such as two-dimensional shapes, was a necessary condition for the development of the notion of conservation of more complex wholes such as continuous quantities with reference to Piaget's experiments on the child's conception of the conservation of liquid.

Introduction

Piaget found that, at one stage of their intellectual development, children are influenced by their immediate perceptual impressions and make their judgements accordingly, that is, by what he called 'global comparison'. He states that a set or collection is only conceivable if it remains unchanged, irrespective of the changes occurring in the relationship between the elements. For instance, the permutations in a given set do not change its value. He also says that a continuous quantity such as length or volume or liquid can only be used in reasoning if it is conceived as being a reconstructible whole and, in fact, the same quantity, irrespective of the possible changes of the parts.

When a child can deal with quantities in this way he has formed the conception of conservation. Piaget found that in order to arrive at this level of understanding, the child had to be able to organise the perceptual changes between the parts in order to arrive at the notion of conservation. He called this operation 'the multiplication of relations' and it is essentially a logical process.

Could the issue be moved back a stage? The elements or parts referred to above are also wholes. Does the child need to have the notion of conservation at a simpler level, that is, the level of the units or parts, before it can deal with permutations, rearrangements of parts or different relationships between these elements?

In order to investigate this, the type of quantity used was a two-dimensional (rigid) shape which could represent a unit or whole and would not involve changes of relationship within itself, as does liquid or collections of beads, and so forth. Shapes such as rectangles, diamonds and ovals, when looked on as quantities, are perceptually analogous to liquids in that the estimation of quantity does involve the two dimensions – height and width.

The hypotheses worked on were:

1. At one stage in the child's development perception would be so dominated by so-called 'global comparisons' that even a two-dimensional shape would not be seen as a constant quantity. Closely related to this would be the inability to perceive the identity of a two-dimensional shape when placed in different orientations.

2. That this stage, i.e. the conservation of two-dimensional shape, would precede the stage of conservation of continuous or discontinuous quantities. In other words, to have formed the conservation of units would be a necessary condition for conservation or continuous or discontinuous quantities.

Choice of subjects

The subjects used for the group of experiments were from two different schools. Group one was from an entrance class of an infants school in the East End, London dock area. The children's ages ranged from two months under five years to five years and three months. Group two was from a working-class area in the centre of London. The average age of this group was five years four months.

In the preliminary experiments forty children were used as subjects. Out of these, a number were not used in the whole series of experiments. The majority of these with whom it was not possible to proceed, for some reason or other, did not become involved in the experimental situation in Stage 1 as they were expected to do. This may have been due to some uneasiness or reserve but, in any case, they showed no real interest. Perhaps they had what Eysenck describes as 'a set to answer all questions in the affirmative.'

On the other hand, there was a minority of children who became so highly involved imaginatively in the situation that the experimental procedure was disorganised. These children thoroughly enjoyed Stage 1 of the first experiment but Stage 2 had to be abandoned.

Experiment 1: Judging relative size of two identical shapes

Apparatus used:

1. Two blue oval shapes – 'Ponds' – made of stiff paper and two paper ducks.

2. Two orange diamond shapes – 'Gardens' – also cut out of stiff paper and two lead figures representing 'ladies gardening'.

3. Two rectangular green shapes – 'Fields' – and two lead horses.

Experiment 2: Perception of identity of shapes

Apparatus used:

1. A sheet of paper on which were drawn six oval shapes in different orientations – one oval in a perpendicular position at the side.

2. A sheet of paper with diamonds instead of ovals in different orientations.

3. A sheet of paper with triangles in different orientations.

Experiment 3: Conservation of liquid

Apparatus used:
Four glasses of equal capacity, two of which were tall and narrow and two, in contrast, were shorter and broader. There was also one jug of orange squash.

Experiment 1

Investigation of the child's conception of conservation of shape based on his judgement of the relative sizes of two shapes when these are moved into different positions. The pattern of the experiment was similar to that used by Piaget in his work on the child's conception of the conservation of liquid.

Stage 1: In order to put the child at ease, objects were introduced in an imaginative way to gain his interest. For example, two small cut-out paper ducks and the two blue oval shapes representing ponds, one for each duck to swim on were shown to the child.

Stage 2: The ducks were then moved to one side, leaving the two oval shapes both in horizontal positions.

The child was then asked to make a judgement about the relative sizes of the two ponds. It was only possible to proceed when the child had judged them to be the same size. To make quite sure about this, two questions were asked: 'Do you think that the ducks have the same amount of water to swim on?' and 'Has one duck got more water than the other?' If the child answered 'yes' to the first question and 'no' to the second, the experiment proceeded.

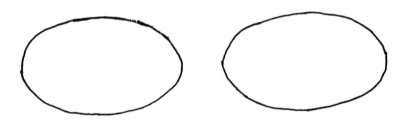

Figure 8.1: Two 'ponds' – First position (both in horizontal positions)
Source: Author

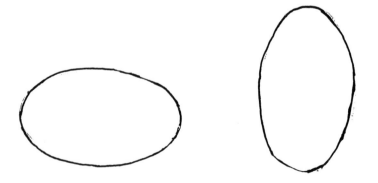

Figure 8.2: Two 'ponds' – Second position (one horizontal, the other vertical)
Source: Author

The two 'ponds' are still both in the horizontal positions and have been judged to be both the same size. One of the ponds is turned round, so it is now looking taller but narrower.

The same questions are asked about the sizes: 'What do you think now?' and 'Are the ponds the same size or is one bigger? The same basic experiment was tried out using the diamond shapes and the rectangles.

Examples of criteria used to assess the child's level of development
Non-conservation of shape. Marion, aged 5 years and 5 months:

1. General talk about ponds and ducks.

2. Marion was asked if the two ponds – in horizontal positions – were as big as each other. She herself turned them both into the perpendicular position and compared them carefully. Her reply to the question was 'yes'. She was asked then if one was bigger. 'No' was her reply.

3. One of the oval shapes was turned through 90 degrees into a horizontal position.

4. 'What do you think now? Pointing at the oval shape in a tall position, she said: 'Like that it is more'.

An example of the achievement of conservation of shape
Janet, aged 5 years:

Having looked at the two oval shapes representing ponds and the two ducks, Janet was asked: 'Have the ducks as much water as each other?' She looked at them very carefully but could not decide. One shape was placed on top of the other and she looked at the edges very carefully. She thought that one was a little bigger at one part of the edge. I cut a little off. She was then satisfied that they were the same. I then asked her if one duck had more water to swim on than the other. She replied: 'No'. The ponds were both still in the horizontal position.

One of the shapes was turned through 90 degrees. Janet was clearly very interested by the perceptual difference. Spontaneously, she said: 'When its like that (pointing at the oval in the tall position) that one is bigger'. But in reply to the question 'Is it more to swim on?', she replied: 'No'. Comparing the two shapes in various positions, her verdict was consistent: 'They both have got the same'.

Two other versions of the above experiment were carried out using diamond shapes (gardens) and rectangular shapes (fields).

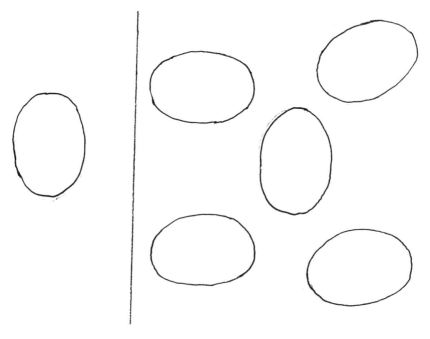

Figure 8.3: Oval shapes in random positions to test shape recognition
Source: Author

Experiment 2

Aim: Investigation of the child's conception of conservation of shape – in terms of his perception of its identity.

Unlike Experiment 1, the shapes were not turned round in front of the child. This time the same shape (either oval, diamond or oblong) was shown in different positions, drawn on a piece of paper. The shapes were called 'egg shape', 'diamond shape' and 'mat shape'. When shown the drawings of the same shape in a number of different positions, how many could be identified as being the same?

Experiment 3: Conservation of liquid

The child's conception of the conservation of liquid. The procedure used was basically the same as described by Piaget (1941) in 'The Child's Conception of Number.' (pp. 3–24)

Results of the three experiments

The test for identity of shape was slightly easier than the tests for conservation of quantity in terms of a non-malleable shape, but conservation of liquid is a more difficult notion to achieve than both.

Tabulated results of the three experiments

f = fail

P = pass

Child's name	Perception of identity	Conservation in relation to shape	Conservation of liquid
1. Rosemary	f	f	f
2. Marion	f	f	f
3. Gillian	f	f	f
4. Susan	f	f	f
5. Paul	f	f	f
6. John	f	f	f
7. Lyn	P	f	f
8. Christine	P	f	f
9. Keith	P	f	f
10. Donald	P	f	f
11. Joan	f	P	f
12. Peter	P	P	f
13. Mary	P	P	f
14. Janet	P	P	f
15. Keith	f	P	P
16. Pauline	P	P	P
17. Pauline	P	P	P
18. Martin	P	P	P
19. James	P	P	P
20. Peter M.	P	P	P

Conclusions

The results supported the hypothesis that there is a stage, prior to the conservation of liquid, at which there is conservation of less complex wholes which might be described as units. To be able to achieve constancy of two-dimensional shapes is a necessary condition for being able to appreciate conservation of liquid.

Before the notion of conservation of shape has developed, ideas about size vary according to changes in visual impressions. Even when the rigid shape is turned round in front of him, the child judges it after each move as though it were a different object. Constancy is a matter of being able to correlate different visual impressions – in other words, generalising the stimuli into a class. Therefore, as one would expect, the ability to conceive of the unchanging size of a shape is related to the ability to perceive the identity of the same shape drawn in different orientations.

The relevance of emotional development to the achievement of an understanding of conservation.

Piaget outlines the development of concepts of conservation underpinning the understanding of number. He does not discuss how this is related to emotional development.

There was a marked discrepancy in performance of Test 1 and 2 in the case of one child, Donald – who also showed signs of emotional disturbance. He asked me questions about how his performance compared with that of other children, and he was clearly anxious about this. Unfortunately, I have no information about Donald's early life (it was outside the scope of this experiment). Subsequently, I was told by the headmistress that he had stolen toys from school and from other children. He suffered from asthma. She also suggested that Donald's mother was unreliable in some way. It is suggested that severe disturbance in early relationships can affect the unfolding of intelligence and a child's ability to think in abstract terms.

References

Anderson, V. and Hood-Williams, J. (n.d.) *Mosaic Test Handbook*. Aylesbury: Lowenfeld Trust.

Bendix, R. and Lipset, S. (1956) *Class Status and Power*. London: Routledge and Kegan Paul Ltd.

Berry, J. (1995) *Hot Earth Cold Earth*. Newcastle: Bloodaxe Books.

Bowlby, J. (1953) *Child Care and the Growth of Love*. London: PelicanBooks.

Brown, J.A.C. (1961) *Freud and the Post-Freudians*. London: PelicanBooks.

Bunyan, J., (1965) *The Pilgrim's Progress*. Harmondsworth: Penguin Classics.

Camus, A., (1942) *The Outsider*. Harmondsworth: Penguin Modern Classics.

Caplan, L. (1979) *Oneness and Separateness*. London: Cape.

Davis, M. and Urwin, C. (1991) *Writings on Lowenfeld*. Cambridge: University of Cambridge. (Lowenfeld Trust 1992)

Fromm, E. (1955) *The Sane Society*. New York: Holt Rinehart and Winston.

Gardiner, N. (1979) *The Burger's Daughter*. London: Jonathan Cape.

Guidano,V F. (1987) *Complexity of the self*. New York: Guilford Press

Guntrip, H. (1968) *Schizoid Phenomena, Object Relations and the Self*. London: Hogarth Press.

Heaney, S. (1991) *Seeing Things*. London: Faber & Faber.

Hodgson Burnett, F. (1975) *The Secret Garden*. London: Dent.

Hugo, V. (1992) *Les Miserables*. New York: Random House.

Hunt, M. (1995) *Real Life*. London: Flamingo, Harper Collins.

James, O. (1997) *Britain on the Couch*. London: Century.

Journal of Psychohistory 20 (1993) New York: The Institute of Psychohistory.

Jung, C G. (1964) *Man and his Symbols*. London: Aldus/Jupiter Books.

Kelley, V.C. (1994) *Leading with my Heart*. New York: Simon and Schuster.

Levi, P. (1979) *The Truce*. London: The Bodley Head.

Lowenfeld, M. (1991) *Play in Childhood*. Aylesbury: Lowenfeld Trust.

Lowenfeld, M. (1977) *The World Technique*. Aylesbury: Lowenfeld Trust.

Lowenfeld, M. (1995) *The Mosaic Test*. Aylesbury: Lowenfeld Trust.

Martin, P. (1997) *The Sickening Mind*. London: Harper Collins.

Masters, B. (1985) *Killing for Company*. London: Coronet Books.

Masters, B. (1993) *The Shrine of Jeffrey Dahmer*. London: Hodder and Stoughton.

Meltzer, D. (1973) *Sexual States of Mind*. Perthshire: Clunie Press.

Meltzer, D. (1975) 'Adhesive Identification', London: Academa Press.

Midgley, M. (1994) *The Ethical Primate*. London: Routledge.

Piaget, J. (1941) *The Child's Conception of Number*. London: Routledge and Kegan Paul Ltd.

Piaget, J. (1947) *The Psychology of Intelligence*. London: Routledge and Kegan Paul Ltd.

Piaget, J. (1954) *The Construction of Reality in the Child*. London: Routledge and Kegan Paul Ltd.

Rycroft, C.F. (1953) 'Some observations on a case of vertigo.' *The International Journal of Psychoanalysis XXXIV*.

Rycroft, C.F. (1968a) *A Critical Dictionary of Psycho-Analysis*. London: Nelson.

Rycroft, C.F. (1968b) *Anxiety and Neurosis*. London: The Penguin Press.

Rycroft, C.F. (1966) *Psychoanalysis Observed*. London: Constable.

Samuels, A. (1993) *The Political Psyche*. London: Routledge.

Shakespeare, W. (1968) *The Merchant of Venice*. London: Macmillan.

Sharrock, R. (1968) *John Bunyan*. London: Macmillan.

Smith, S. (1964) 'Not Waving, but Drowning' from *Selected Poems*. London: Longman Group Ltd.

Thompson, D'Arcy Wentworth. (1942) *On Growth and Form*. Cambridge: Cambridge University Press.

Tustin, F. (1972) *Autism and Childhood Psychosis*. London: Hogarth Press.

Winnicott, D.W. (1958) *Through Paediatrics to Psycho-analysis*. London: Hogarth Press.

Winnicott, D.W. (1964) *The Child, 0the Family and the Outside World*. London: Pelican.

Winnicott, D.W. (1974) *Playing and Reality*. Harmondsworth: Penguin.

Subject Index

Author Index